51-60
74-94 } ①

112-128? plus dogmatics

NATURAL THEOLOGY

NATURAL THEOLOGY

Comprising "Nature and Grace" by
Professor Dr. EMIL BRUNNER and the
reply "No!" by Dr. KARL BARTH

Translated from the German by PETER FRAENKEL

With an Introduction by

The Very Rev. Professor JOHN BAILLIE, D.D., D.LITT.

Wipf and Stock Publishers
EUGENE, OREGON

Fisrt published 1946

Wipf and Stock Publishers
199 West 8th Avenue, Suite 3
Eugene, Oregon 97401

Natural Theology
Comprising "Nature and Grace" by Professor Dr. Emil Brunner and the
reply "No!" by Dr. Karl Barth
By Brunner, Dr. Emil and Barth, Dr. Karl
Copyright© 2002,   TVZ and Mohr Siebeck
ISBN: 1-59244-112-2
Publication Date: December, 2002,
Previously published by Geoffrey Bles: The Centenary Press.

Karl Barth *"Nein! Antwort an Emil Brunner"* copyright © of
the German original version, Theologischer Verlag Zürich.

Emil Brunner: *Natur und Gnade* copyright© of the German
original version, Mohr Siebeck.

INTRODUCTION

By The Very Rev. Professor JOHN BAILLIE, D.D., D.Litt.

THE remarkable pair of brochures which Mr. Peter Fraenkel here places at the disposal of English readers appeared in the original German in 1934 and quickly attracted the most widespread attention. They were accepted as giving definitive, if not classical, expression to what was at that time beginning to emerge as a burning issue in Protestant theology, and they at once became the subject of keen debate not only in continental Europe but also in great Britain and America. The English translation has been too long delayed, yet it is likely to be greeted with hardly lessened interest, since the controversy is still carried on with unabated vigour.

When Dr. Barth and Dr. Brunner were first heard of in the English-speaking world they were regarded as representing an identical point of view—the point of view variously spoken of as the Barthian theology, the theology of crisis, and the dialectical theology. It would seem that this was at the time a sufficiently correct impression, and one likely to be assented to by the writers themselves; for, as Dr. Barth indicates in the present brochure, it was "roughly after 1929" that a divergence began to manifest itself. If it be asked what it was which up to that time the two theologians seemed to be saying in common, and which had not been said before (or was not then in the habit of being said) in quite the same way, the answer is probably to be found in their united insistence that not only is there no salvation, but there is also no true knowledge of God, save in and through Jesus Christ. The idea of the total corruption of human nature, strongly entrenched in orthodox Protestantism but lately fallen into disrepute, was now not only vigorously reaffirmed by both writers, but was given an application even more extended than orthodoxy had usually given it; this total corruption being made so to cover the human reason as to render men incapable of reaching any knowledge of God by the exercise of their own powers of thought, or even of bringing them to a point in their thinking such as would enable them to welcome the Christian revelation, when it came, as answering a question they had already raised or meeting a need they had already felt. The Word of God in Christ came "vertically from above" into the existing human situation and appeared only as foolishness to the best of human wisdom. It did, indeed, meet with a response from those elected to respond to it, but this response was not on the ground of anything already present in their souls; rather did the revelation create its own response.

It is within this circle of common ideas that the issue between the disputants is now joined. These ideas are themselves so far from being accepted by many British and American theologians that the difference between Dr. Barth and Dr. Brunner may seem to some to be of small consequence in comparison with the extensive ground they occupy in common—an impression of a kind which is very frequently received by those who survey even the most heated controversies from a point widely distant in time or in tradition. The very fervid heat with which this controversy is carried on (especially in Dr. Barth's contribution to it, from his "Angry Introduction" onwards) will therefore be surprising to many English readers. It may even be shocking to them. The bitterness which has ever characterised theological discussion both in Germany itself and in other German-speaking continental lands has

long been foreign to our English-speaking tradition. It
is to be hoped that it will remain foreign, but it is equally
to be hoped that it will not in this instance prove a
barrier to the appreciation of the importance of the
questions with which our continental friends are concerned. They themselves would no doubt claim that
the difference in manner is due largely to the difference
in our respective situations. We can afford to discuss
calmly matters which to them, living as they have
recently done in an atmosphere of religious persecution,
have beeñ concerns of life and death in the most literal
sense. Nor will any of us wish to deny all validity to
this claim, whether or not it be accepted as a complete
explanation. At all events the fact would seem to be
that the controversy which made its first full-dress
appearance in these pages, still rages as bitterly as ever;
and we are informed that in the Switzerland to which
both disputants are native, and in which both now
teach, there are not many students or amateurs of
theology who do not definitely know on which side they
stand.

In 1935 Dr. Brunner published a second and con-
siderably enlarged edition of his brochure, and the
question had accordingly to be faced which of the two
editions should now be translated. German-speaking
scholars in the fields of philosophy and theology are
very much in the habit of publishing successive editions
of their works, which are not merely reprints but are
marked by substantial alterations and additions. Almost
always it is the latest available edition that is chosen
for translation into other tongues, since it is naturally
taken to represent the most recent and considered
opinions of the author. In the present case, however,
another counsel had to be followed, since Dr. Barth's
reply to Dr. Brunner was being translated as a com-
panion piece. It was the first edition of Dr. Brunner's

pamphlet that Dr. Barth had before him when he wrote
his reply, and Dr. Brunner's second edition already
takes notice of this reply; so that Dr. Barth could not be
expected to agree to his own pamphlet appearing as a
reply to a statement which had been altered after he
had replied to it. It is therefore the first edition of
Nature and Grace which Mr. Fraenkel has here translated
for us.

Nevertheless, in fairness to Dr. Brunner, some further
explanation must be made. He was careful to let the
text of his first edition, so far as it went, stand unaltered
in the second, aside from minor corrections. Of these
minor corrections none is worthy of notice save the
footnotes giving the volume and page references for a
number of his quotations from Calvin, which were at
first given wrongly. The new references he has been
conscientious enough to mark with an asterisk to show
their divergence from those given in the first edition, but
Mr. Fraenkel has rightly substituted the correct references for the earlier incorrect ones. What is new in Dr.
Brunner's second edition is a Foreword of seven pages
together with some sixteen pages of explanatory notes
at the end. In no part of this additional matter does
Dr. Brunner think of himself as countering Dr. Barth's
charges, his professed anxiety being merely to correct
some of the latter's misunderstandings of the words he
had used and the position he had defended; it being as
important to Dr. Barth as to himself that such verbal
barriers should be cleared away and the real difference
between them accurately understood. Dr. Brunner
allows that he may himself have had some share of the
blame for some of these misunderstandings, but he
points out that in one important instance Dr. Barth
has been guilty of actual misquotation. In *Nature and
Grace* it is frequently affirmed that even fallen man
retains *Wortmächtigkeit*, which Mr. Fraenkel translates

as "capacity for words," but which might have been
translated a little less literally as "capacity for speech."
But Dr. Barth in his reply constantly seems to attribute
to Dr. Brunner the use of the word *Offenbarungsmächtigkeit* in this connection, *i.e.* "capacity for revelation."
This substitution is no doubt to be explained by the
fact that "the Word" is a familiar synonym for revelation, so that the two compound terms might appear to
be exact equivalents. But Dr. Brunner professes as great
a horror as had done his opponent at the idea that man
has a "capacity for revelation," if this be understood
in the active sense of having any control over it, any
part (as it were) in the revealing. The capacity he
claims for man is, he explains, the purely passive capacity
to be reached by the revelation and to hear the Word
when it is uttered.

A further explanation made by Dr. Brunner concerns
his use of the term "natural theology." He distinguishes
between an objective sense of the term, which he accepts,
and a subjective sense, which he rejects. By the former
he means such a knowledge of God in his creation as
can come only to those who are already enlightened
by the Christian revelation of him; by the latter he
means such a knowledge of God as might be supposed
to be accessible to the heathen or to independent rational
argumentation. And he professes himself ready, in
order to avoid further misunderstanding, to drop the
term "natural theology" altogether, substituting for it
such a phrase as "the Christian doctrine of general
revelation or of revelation in nature."

In view of Dr. Brunner's willingness to let the first
edition of his brochure be translated instead of the
second, it is no less than just to him that these later
explanations should be at the disposal of the English
reader. Moreover it seems right also to set out in
translation the following passage from the Foreword to

his second edition, though the reader should keep in mind that it is *subsequent* to Dr. Barth's reply, and should strictly have appeared at the end rather than at the beginning of the present volume.

Dr. Brunner asks why it is that St. Paul, who had nothing to proclaim but "Jesus Christ and him crucified," should begin the exposition of his message in the Epistle to the Romans by a twofold reference to the revelation of God in nature. The answer, he says, is not very difficult.

"Before the Apostle further unfolds and elaborates the message which he has clearly presented in the opening verses of the first chapter like the theme of a fugue, he settles accounts with himself and his readers concerning the situation of the men to whom the message is addressed. Here he lays the foundation stone of a Christian doctrine concerning 'natural man,' and of a Christian doctrine of heathen religion. For he knows that faith inevitably forms and develops itself in the heart of man in such a way as to constrain him to a critical self-understanding on the part of unbelieving 'natural' man. This is nothing but the twofold occurrence of 'repentance' and 'trust'; saying No to oneself in saying Yes to the saving grace of God. The quintessence of this settling of accounts thus lies in the one word 'inexcusable' (Romans ii. 1). Hence these two chapters deal with the responsibility of the ungodly for their ungodliness. But the ground of this imputation of responsibility lies in the doctrine of general revelation or revelation in nature. The godlessness of the natural man does not mean that God stands apart from him—for the Creator has truly not left himself without witness among his creatures—but consists in the fact that man has *perverted* what he has and knows of God (Romans i. 23), that he turns himself away from the God who so mightily declares himself, and uses the revelation in creation in order to reverence the creature rather than the Creator. Accordingly 'the heathen' do not stand outside the revelation of God, or out of relation to him; they stand rather in that *alienatio originis* which from the human side must be called sin and from the divine side the wrath of God.

"The knowledge of this fact is of decisive importance for this missionary to the heathen who has set the standard for all ages; and it ought to be of decisive importance, now as then, for all who proclaim the Gospel. It concerns the responsibility, which has a double grounding in the revelation in creation, of the man who is to be reached by the Gospel. This knowledge becomes practically effective in the 'contact,' indispensable for every missionary, between his proclamation of Christ and the revelation of God (which leaves men inexcusable) in the works of creation and in the law written in the heart. The classical examples of this are to be found in the only two missionary discourses which the New Testament has handed down to us in any detail—in the fourteenth and seventeenth chapters of the Acts of the Apostles. No missionary has ever preached, or can preach, otherwise than thus: the God whom ye, perverted by your sinful blindness, unknowingly worship as the unknown, him do I proclaim to you as he who has 'made known the secret of his will' to us in Jesus Christ the Crucified and Risen.

"He who thinks as a missionary, understands without further ado the central significance of this contact, normative and productive of repentance, with the twofold revelation in creation; and he knows also that far from prejudicing the *sola gratia*, it alone makes possible the preaching of justification. Everything depends on the establishment of this responsibility, which makes men guilty; and the responsibility itself depends on the reality of a general revelation in creation which precedes the revelation of reconciliation in Jesus Christ, and indeed precedes all historical life."

It remains only to add that in the years which have passed since 1934 both disputants have taken occasion to set out their views in much greater detail. From Dr. Barth we have had several volumes of his monumental *Kirchliche Dogmatik*, following on the rewritten first half-volume which was englished by Professor G. T. Thomson in 1936—*The Doctrine of the Word of God*. From Dr. Brunner we have had *Wahrheit als Begegnung* (1938), translated into English as *The Divine-Human Encounter* by Dr. Amandus W. Loos (1944); and, even more important, *Offenbarung und Vernunft* (1941), which has been translated by Miss Olive Wyon and now awaits publication—no doubt under the title *Revelation and Reason*. The study of these larger works will greatly clarify the student's mind as to the exact nature of the divergence between the two disputants, and may also be expected to contribute something to the answering of the further and more important questions: Which of them is right? Or, if neither is entirely right, which of them comes nearer the truth, and where exactly does each go astray? And may there even be something amiss with the ground they occupy in common?

TRANSLATOR'S NOTE

THE text of the essay *Nature and Grace* is that of the first edition; the references to Calvin's *Institutes*, however, are taken from the revised second edition. Those marked with an asterisk appear (thus) in the second edition only.

The discussion turns in part on the meaning of the term *Offenbarungsmächtigkeit*. This has been rendered by "capacity for revelation" as being capable, like the German, both of an active and of a passive interpretation.

The usual translation of the technical term "Ordnung" —"order" has been replaced by "ordinance." The term refers, of course, to the natural, not to the revealed, law. It is much to be hoped that this usage, for which there is precedent in the English language, will supersede the former, for which there is none.

The translator's thanks are due in various ways to the Rev. H. Cunliffe-Jones, the Rev. A. Whitehouse and the Rev. A. R. Vidler, O.G.S.; also to the two authors for so kindly answering the questions put to them concerning the text.

P. F.

NATURE AND GRACE

A Contribution to the Discussion with Karl Barth by
E. BRUNNER, D.D., *Professor of Theology at Zurich*

IT has been frequently suggested to me during recent
months that it was time for me to write a polemical
treatise against Karl Barth. And not without reason.
Even before his great purge, in which the valuable
periodical *Zwischen den Zeiten* was eliminated, he repre-
sented me to his readers as a thoroughly unreliable
theologian who showed treacherous inclinations both
towards Thomism and towards Neo-Protestantism. This
created a painful confusion in the minds of those who
had until then believed us to be loyal comrades in
arms.[1] Our good friends abroad who were accustomed to mention Barth's name and mine in one
breath were however to hear yet stranger things. In
the work in which he disowned (we might as well
say) all other theologians, Barth's ban struck me also.[2]
Now I belong to the unpleasant category of neutrals
who are neither hot nor cold, who say neither entirely
Yes nor entirely No.

In all this my fate has been rather strange. Certainly
what my friend Barth wrote concerning me did not
please me, yet I was quite unable to be angry with him
on that account. Not because I am such a good Christian
and bless those that curse me, but simply because in
spite of it all and above all else I was so pleased with
everything else that Karl Barth did and wrote, that I
pocketed also what he wrote against me—though of
course unwillingly. But this is not all. I feel myself so
much an ally of Barth even in what he believed that
he had to say against me, that I was able to take the

misunderstanding fairly lightly. Barth appeared to me like a loyal soldier on sentry duty at night, who shoots every one who does not give him the password as he has been commanded, and who therefore from time to time also annihilates a good friend whose password he does not hear or misunderstands in his eagerness. As far as I was concerned he missed; but I cannot be angry at his desired attempt, as I am unable to find any ill-will in it.

Therefore it is far from my mind to write a polemical treatise, although in itself, as some people know, this would not be a new undertaking to me. Rather is it my purpose to show in this pamphlet the following three things: that what Barth really desires and intends, and for which in this last decisive year he has so bravely and far-sightedly contended, is what I also desire and intend, and for which I also strove to work with my more modest powers; but that from what he rightly desires and intends he draws false conclusions; and thirdly, that he is wrong in accusing of treason to the essentials those who are not willing to join him in drawing these conclusions. In spite of long and honest attempts I have failed to convince my friend of the correctness of my tenets and therefore I have had to have recourse to a public disputation. For I am not only concerned to clear my theology of the charge which Barth has preferred against it, but above all to help to overcome the deadlock and the petrifaction in false antitheses which threatens the theological discussion because of Barth's one-sidedness.

I

THE ISSUE BETWEEN KARL BARTH AND MYSELF

THE credit of having given back to Protestant theology its proper theme and subject-matter is due, without qualification and, if I may use the expression, without competition, to Karl Barth. It is not as though there were not before him, and to some extent beside him, men who also knew the proper theme and subject. Men like Adolf Schlatter and, above all, Martin Kaehler[3] did not wish to do anything but bring to bear the pure and undiluted message of the Bible upon the doctrines of the Church. But they were unable to break through the front of theological modernism. A task such as this demanded greater mental impetus and this Karl Barth possessed. Within the space of a few years he completely changed the Protestant theological situation. Even where he was not acknowledged, his influence was very considerable. To-day we struggle no longer, as we did fifteen years ago, concerning "religion," but concerning the "Word of God"; no longer concerning the *deus in nobis*, but concerning the revelation in Jesus Christ. To put it briefly: no longer concerning the themes of the enlightenment, but concerning the theme of the Bible itself. We others who have assisted Barth in this struggle have all of us first had our eyes opened by him, even though some have never publicly acknowledged Barth.

But the fact that we are to-day again concerned with the message of the Bible and the Reformation is not all. The seriousness with which Barth takes his mission is shown by the fact that he was not satisfied with this first

victory, but on the contrary now employed all his powers
the more. The most recent developments have shown
how right he was in regarding the general talk about
the theology of the Reformation and the general appeal
to Luther not only as of no value but as dangerous.
We are not concerned with Luther nor with Lutheranism,
but with that hard truth and message of Luther's concerning *sola gratia*, which is so greatly opposed to the
thought of our time—with Christ crucified as the only
salvation of the world and with justification by faith
alone. We are concerned with the doctrine that in all
questions of the Church's proclamation Holy Scripture
alone is the ultimate standard. We are concerned with
the message of the sovereign, freely electing grace of
God. Of his free mercy God gives to man, who of himself
can do nothing towards his own salvation, to man,
whose will is not free but in bondage, his salvation in the
Cross of Christ and by the Holy Spirit who enables him
to assimilate this word of the Cross. We are therefore
also concerned with the freedom of the Church, which
has its basis and its justification, its law and its possibility purely and solely in this divine revelation. Therefore it is not tied at all to nations and states. It is above
all nations and states without any possibility of accepting
from them any law or commission. We are concerned
with the fact that the proclamation of the Church has
not two sources and norms, such as *e.g.* revelation *and*
reason or the Word of God *and* history, and that ecclesiastical or Christian action has not two norms, such as
e.g. commandments *and* "Ordinances." The struggle
against this "and"[4] is the struggle of Elijah on Mount
Carmel against the halting between two opinions and
therefore it is the struggle for the glory of the true God.
In all this there is between me and Barth no difference of
opinion, except the one on the side of Barth that there is
a difference of opinion. All I can say is: No, there is

none. The title of my book,[5] *Das Gebot und die Ordnungen*, may seem to contradict this, but this is purely an appearance and is of no more significance than Barth's title to an essay on an analogous theme, "Kirche und Kultur." It is an "and" denoting a problem, a relation to be investigated, not an "and" of co-ordination. But for the moment we may point to the fact that there is indeed here a serious problem, by quoting what Luther said at the Diet of Worms: if he were not overcome "by testimony of Holy Writ or clear reason" (*ratione evidente*), he would not recant. Not even Karl Barth can deny that there is a *problem* concerning Christianity and Culture, Commandment and Ordinances, Reason and Revelation, and that this problem requires thoroughgoing theological treatment.

II

BARTH'S FALSE CONCLUSIONS

I HAVE repeatedly pointed out that most theology is made necessary by heretics using the terms of the true faith, while meaning by them something other than the plain words can signify.[6] Not open heresy but hidden heresy is the real danger in the Church; it is the internal enemy, ever more dangerous than the external. Hence it is understandable that suspicion belongs as it were to the professional virtues of the good theologian. It is a fact that he is called to be a guardian, and as the bodyguard of any great man of this world look upon every one who is near him with suspicion until they have convinced themselves of his harmlessness, so also the theologian must act—not as a man but as a bearer of his office. Therefore I cannot agree with those who reproach

Barth with this "heresy-hunting." It is the result of his great devotion to his subject, and this not even his most embittered adversaries have been able to deny him. If I reproach Barth with anything at all it is with this, that he would like it best to carry out this guardian's duty alone, and that if anyone wishes to call his attention to a mistake he is not ready to believe that he, Barth, could be in error; and that in this matter he puts into practice the not very biblical maxim of William Tell that "the strong man is strongest alone." Apart from that the difference between us is purely objective and theological and can only be removed if we test it anew by that standard which we both acknowledge.

From the doctrine of *sola gratia* and the position of the Bible as the sole ultimate standard of truth Barth draws the following conclusions:

(1) Since man is a sinner who can be saved only by grace, the image of God in which he was created is obliterated entirely, *i.e.* without remnant. Man's rational nature, his capacity for culture and his humanity, none of which can be denied, contain no traces or remnants whatever of that lost image of God.

(2) Since we acknowledge scriptural revelation as the sole norm of our knowledge of God and the sole source of our salvation, every attempt to assert a "general revelation" of God in nature, in the conscience and in history, is to be rejected outright. There is no sense in acknowledging two kinds of revelation, one general and one special. There is only one kind, namely the one complete revelation in Christ.

(3) Accordingly we have to draw the following conclusion from the acknowledgment of Christ as the sole saving grace of God: there is no grace of creation and preservation active from the creation of the world and apparent to us in God's preservation of the world. For otherwise we would have to acknowledge two or even

three kinds of grace, and this would contradict the oneness of the grace of Christ.

(4) Accordingly there is no such thing as God's ordinances of preservation, which we could know to be such and in which we could recognise the will of God which is normative of our own action. A *lex naturae* of this kind which is derived from creation can be introduced into Christian theology only *per nefas*, as a pagan thought.

(5) For the same reason it is not permissible to speak of the "point of contact" for the saving action of God. For this would contradict the sole activity of the saving grace of Christ, which is the centre of the theology of the Bible and the Reformation.

(6) Similarly the new creation is in no wise a perfection of the old, but comes into being exclusively through destruction of the old and is a replacement of the old man by the new. The sentence, *gratia non tollit naturam sed perficit*, is in no sense correct, but is altogether an arch heresy.

We could cite many similarly derived theses from other departments of theology, *e.g.* from the doctrine of the new birth, of sanctification, from the doctrine of faith and works, etc. I confine myself to those which have stood in the centre of the latest discussions. They are all connected with the problem of *theologia naturalis*, the first four directly, the fifth and sixth indirectly.

Karl Barth characterises the errors attacked in these theses with various names of heretics taken from the history of dogma. But we can sum up his characterisations under three specially significant heads: the "errors" rejected in these theses are, firstly, unbiblical; secondly, Thomistic and Roman Catholic and therefore against the Reformation; and thirdly, derived from the Enlightenment and Neo-Protestantism and *therefore* against the Reformation.

As Karl Barth has expounded and defended these theses only incidentally and never systematically, or rather has only thus attacked the counter-theses,[7] we submit these formulations of his opinions to his correction. I have formulated them as Barth's opinions as best I can. I am not perfectly certain, however, whether I have hit upon every shade of Barth's opinion.

In what follows I set out:

(1) My counter-theses with a very brief scriptural proof.

(2) A discussion of its relation in the history of dogma to the Reformation, to Thomism and to Neo-Protestantism.

(3) A concluding discussion of the theological and practical significance of the controversy, *i.e.* of the interest of theology and the Church in the rejection of the conclusions which Barth draws from his correct fundamental position.

III

MY COUNTER-THESES AND THEIR PROOF

(1) THE question concerning the *imago Dei* seems to be ultimately nothing but a dispute about words. I agree with Barth in teaching that the original image of God in man has been destroyed, that the *justitia originalis* has been lost and with it the possibility of doing or even of willing to do that which is good in the sight of God, and that therefore the free will has been lost. Barth himself does not deny that even sinful and unredeemed man is capable of doing and thinking what is reasonable, and that in spite of their questionable nature humanity and culture are not simply to be dismissed as of no value

from the point of view of revelation. It might therefore
appear as of no account whether we would connect these
abilities, which even natural man has, with the original
image of God or not. Why should we be concerned to
introduce here the dangerous and vague concept of the
remnant of the *imago*? We shall discuss the purpose of
this in the last chapter. Here I shall justify myself by
saying the following:

We have to consider the image of God in man in two
ways: one formal and one material. The formal sense of
the concept is the human, *i.e.* that which distinguishes
man from all the rest of creation, whether he be a sinner
or not. Even the Old Testament speaks of man's likeness
to God in this sense. It signifies above all the superiority
of man within creation. Thus in the two important
passages (Genesis i. 26 and Ps. viii.) man has not, even
as a sinner, ceased to be the central and culminating
point of creation. This superior position in the whole of
creation, which man still has, is based on his special
relation to God, *i.e.* on the fact that God has created
him for a special purpose—to bear his image. This
function or calling as a bearer of the image is not only
not abolished by sin; rather is it the presupposition of the
ability to sin and continues within the state of sin. We
can define this by two concepts: the fact that man is a
subject and his responsibility. Man has an immeasurable
advantage over all other creatures, even as a sinner, and
this he has in common with God: he is a subject, a
rational creature. The difference is only that God is the
original, man a derived subject. Not even as a sinner
does he cease to be one with whom one can speak, with
whom therefore also God can speak. And this is the very
nature of man: to be responsible. Even as a sinner man
is responsible. Upon these two characteristics, that of
his capacity for words and that of responsibility, which in
their turn are closely interrelated, depends not only

man's special position but also the connection between this special position and the form of the redeeming revelation, namely that God becomes man.

If the formal side of the *imago Dei* is thus conceived, it does not in any way result in an encroachment upon the material concept of *justitia originalis*, nor in a lessening of the weight of the statement that this *justitia originalis* is completely lost.[8] Therefore we do not use the questionable concept of the "remnant" which would suggest a quantitative and therefore relative concept of sin. We distinguish categorically: formally the *imago* is not in the least touched—whether sinful or not, man is a subject and is responsible. Materially the *imago* is completely lost, man is a sinner through and through and there is nothing in him which is not defiled by sin. To formulate it differently: as before, man is a person, *i.e.* he is in a derived sense that which God is originally. Yet he is not a personal person but an anti-personal person; for the truly personal is existence in love, the submission of the self to the will of God and therefore an entering into communion with one's fellow-creature because one enjoys communion with God. This *quid* of personality is negatived through sin, whereas the *quod* of personality constitutes the *humanum* of every man, also that of the sinner.

(2) The world is the creation of God. In every creation the spirit of the creator is in some way recognisable. The artist is known by all his works. So much do the Scriptures of the Old and New Testament testify to the fact that this applies also in our world, which is the stage on which we sinful creatures act, that it is unnecessary to quote any special passages in support. The praise of God through his creation is also an integral part of the Christian liturgy from the earliest times and throughout all centuries. Scripture itself says so and upbraids man for not acknowledging it, and it expects

from him as a believer that he should take part in this
praise of God through his creation. Therefore it seems
to me a queer kind of loyalty to Scripture to demand
that such a revelation should not be acknowledged, in
order that the significance of biblical revelation should
not be minimised.

Wherever God does anything, he leaves the imprint
of his nature upon what he does. Therefore the creation
of the world is at the same time a revelation, a self-
communication of God. This statement is not pagan but
fundamentally Christian. But nowhere does the Bible
give any justification for the view that through the sin
of man this perceptibility of God in his works is destroyed,
although it is adversely affected. Rather does it say this,
that surprisingly enough sin makes man blind for what
is visibly set before our eyes. The reason why men are
without excuse is that they will not know the God who
so clearly manifests himself to them.[9]

The same is true of what is usually called "conscience,"
i.e. of the consciousness of responsibility. Men have not
only responsibility but also consciousness of it—which
could be shown by a more detailed phenomenological
analysis to be necessarily interconnected. Only because
men somehow know the will of God are they able to sin. ·
A being which knew nothing of the law of God would
be unable to sin—as we see in the case of animals.
Responsibility of the sinner and knowledge of the will of
God as the source of law (the knowledge also being
derived from the law) are one and the same thing. We
are not concerned here to discuss what value this legal
knowledge of God has. Scripture clearly testifies to the
fact that knowledge of the law of God is somehow also
knowledge of God.[10] We shall discuss the revelation of
God in history later.

The question can be raised whether it is not necessary
to modify this clear doctrine of Scripture in view of the

knowledge which we have gained in these days. Just as we are driven by St. Paul to a more profound grasping of the problem of the knowledge of God from law and from grace, so also we have the impression of the revelation of God in Scripture as a whole, that this simple doctrine of God as the artificer-demiurge needs further theological treatment. But that is a separate matter, and whatever may be the solution of the second question, we cannot doubt that this simple, universal Christian opinion is scriptural.

The difficult question is therefore not whether there are two kinds of revelation. The reply to this question must on the basis of Scripture once and for all be a positive one. The question is rather how the two revelations, that in creation and that in Jesus Christ, are related. The first answer—again one which is universally Christian and also obviously biblical—is that for us sinful men, the first, the revelation in creation, is not sufficient in order to know God in such a way that this knowledge brings salvation. Furthermore, we have to make the significant distinction between the subjective and the objective factor in this interrelation of knowledge. According to St. Paul the revelation of God in his creation would be sufficient for every one to know therein the Creator according to his majesty and wisdom. But sin dulls man's sight so much that instead of God he "knows" or "fancies" gods. We may correctly characterise the objective and subjective factors thus: man misrepresents the revelation of God in creation and turns it into idols. In any case he is unable to know God, who in Jesus Christ reveals himself to him anew according to his true nature, which even in creation is partially hidden.

But in faith, taking our stand upon the revelation in Jesus Christ, we shall not be able to avoid speaking of a double revelation: of one in creation[11] which only he can recognise in all its magnitude, whose eyes have been opened by Christ; and of a second in Jesus Christ in whose bright light he can clearly perceive the former. This latter revelation far surpasses that which the former was able to show him, and moreover it points to a third revelation, the beatific vision, which again will be entirely different from the second and yet will not deny it, but only confer upon it its ineffable perfection.

This means that in the phrase "natural revelation" the word "natural" is to be understood in a double sense, one objective-divine and one subjective-human-sinful.

The term "nature" can be applied to such permanent capacity for revelation as God has bestowed upon his works, to the traces of his own nature which he has expressed and shown in them.

But the term "nature" can also be applied to what sinful man makes of this in his ignorant knowledge, just as it can be applied to that which God has implanted in human nature as an image of himself, indestructible, yet always obscured by sin. Or it can be applied to what man himself makes of himself through sin. Therefore one can say in conclusion: Only the Christian, i.e. the man who stands within the revelation in Christ, has the true natural knowledge of God.

All these concepts need further theological consideration. But such consideration cannot alter these fundamental outlines without contradicting the testimony of Scripture. Even the most perfect theology will in the main be unable to get beyond the double statement that as concerns the heathen, God did not leave himself without witness,[12] but that nevertheless they did not know him in such a way that he became their salvation.

(3) Wherever both the omnipotent creator and sin are taken equally seriously, there must needs arise a third concept, that of God's gracious preservation. God is present even to his sinful creature which is far removed

from him. This incongruence of divine presence and human distance is highly important. It appears in the double concept of nature which has already been mentioned. The manner in which God is present to his fallen creature is his *preserving grace*. Preserving grace does not abolish sin but abolishes the worst consequences of sin. The grace of preservation for the most part consists in that God does not entirely withdraw his grace of creation from the creature in spite of the latter's sin. In part, however, in that, agreeably to the state of sin, he provides new means for checking the worst consequences of sin, *e.g.* the State.

Preserving grace is a concept of quite undoubted biblical dignity. It is necessary to emphasise this specially, as it is in a manner of speaking a dangerous concept, for from it our thinking can easily slip into a pantheistic doctrine of immanence. What was said above of the revelation in creation is valid here also, viz. that only in the light of the revelation in Christ is it possible to speak correctly of preserving grace. But the Christian is now under the serious obligation to speak of it—by way of thanksgiving. That God is so good that he makes his sun to shine on the evil and on the good . . ., that he gives us life, health, strength, etc.—in short the whole sphere of natural life and its goods—all that must be included in the concept of preserving grace or—as it is therefore called—*general grace*. In the faith of Christ we know that even before we knew the saving grace of God, we lived by the grace of God, *i.e.* by the preserving grace of God, without properly knowing it.

Together with the whole of natural life we must include in this sphere also the whole of historical life, for in man these two are inseparable. In faith not only what we derive from our parents, but also what we derive from our people and their history, the benefits which form the historical inheritance of the whole of mankind, are seen to be given by the preserving grace of God. Consequently human activity comes within the purview of divine grace—not of redeeming but of preserving grace.[13] All activity of man which the creator himself uses to preserve his creation amid the corruptions of sin belongs to this type of activity within preserving grace. It is from this that the doctrine of civil and secular functions and offices is derived.

How integral a part the doctrine of preserving grace forms in the whole of biblical theology is shown by the fact that it is clearly and diligently taught in the Old and even in the New Testament, in spite of the eschatological high tension which emphasises above all the present world's need of redemption and its opposition to God. Accordingly Christian piety has throughout all ages praised this preserving grace of God in hymn and prayer, and the Church has always seen in it a criterion of true faith.

(4) Within the sphere of this preserving grace belong above all those "ordinances" which are the constant factors of historical and social life, and which therefore form a basic part of all ethical problems. There are certain ordinances, such as e.g. Matrimony and the State, without which no communal life is conceivable, that could in any way be termed human. These ordinances vary in dignity.

Monogamous marriage, for example, is of higher dignity than the State because, as an institution, as an ordinance, it is—apart from special concrete cases— unrelated to sin. (This is independent of the way in which its humane necessity may be proved, i.e. is made known to us.) Therefore it has from of old been called an "ordinance of creation." This means simply that the Christian, who recognises the creator only in Jesus Christ, also recognises the ordinance of matrimony to have been instituted by the creator. The distinction

between this "ordinance of creation" from a mere
"ordinance of preservation" relative to sin, such as the
State, is made for sound theological reasons. It is
necessary for a Christian *theologia naturalis, i.e.* for Christian
theological thinking which tries to account for the
phenomena of natural life. Matrimony is a "natural"
ordinance of the creator because the possibility of and
the desire for its realisation lies within human nature
and because it is realised to some extent by men who
are ignorant of the God revealed in Christ.

For this reason there lies over these ordinances a
twilight which cannot be dispelled. They are given by
God. They are realised naturally. For their realisation
not only the natural impulse is necessary but also the
humanum. They can be recognised as necessities and
as goods by natural man. But—and this is the critical
point: only by means of faith can their significance be
perfectly understood and therefore it is only by means of
faith that they can be realised according to the will of
him who has instituted them. Nevertheless, *i.e.* although
they are understood correctly only in faith, they are and
remain for the believer divine ordinances of *nature.* This
means that they do not belong to the realm of redemption, of the Church, but belong to the realm of divine
preservation, in which natural impulse and reason are
constituent factors. All human arts by which man,
thanks to the divine grace of preservation, maintains
himself, are performed by instinct or by reason. Similarly all these ordinances, whether they be "ordinances
of creation" or "ordinances of preservation" in the
narrower sense, are created and maintained by instinct
and reason. Even the believer, who by reason of his
faith understands their ultimate sense better than the
unbeliever, cannot but allow his instinct and his reason
to function with regard to these ordinances, just as in
the arts. And finally it is true that only by means of

faith, *i.e.* through Christ, their relation to the loving will of God can be rightly understood. Nevertheless through the preserving grace of God they are known also to "natural man" as ordinances that are necessary and somehow holy and are by him respected as such. For it is peculiar to the preserving grace of God that he does his preserving work both by nature acting unconsciously and by the reason of man.

(5) No one who agrees that only human subjects but not stocks and stones can receive the Word of God and the Holy Spirit can deny that there is such a thing as a point of contact for the divine grace of redemption. This point of contact is the formal *imago Dei*, which not even the sinner has lost, the fact that man is man, the *humanitas* in the two meanings defined above: capacity for words and responsibility. Not even sin has done away with the fact that man is receptive of words, that he and he alone is receptive of the Word of God. But this "receptivity" must not be understood in the material sense. This receptivity says nothing as to his acceptance or rejection of the Word of God. It is the purely formal possibility of his being addressed.

This possibility of his being addressed is also the presupposition of man's responsibility. Only a being that can be addressed is responsible, for it alone can make decisions. Only a being that can be addressed is capable of sin. But in sinning, while being responsible, it somehow or other knows of its sin. This knowledge of sin is a necessary presupposition of the understanding of the divine message of grace. It will not do to kill the dialectic of this knowledge of sin by saying that knowledge of sin comes only by the grace of God. This statement is as true as the other, that the grace of God is comprehensible only to him who already knows about sin. The case is similar to that of the divine ordinances or of the law: Natural man knows them and yet does not know them.

If he did not know them, he would not be human: if he really knew them, he would not be a sinner. This dichotomy is itself the essence of the state of sin. *Without* knowledge of God there can be no sin: sin is always "in the sight of God." *In* sin there can be no knowledge of God, for the true knowledge of God is the abolition of sin. This dialectic must not be one-sidedly abolished. On the contrary it must be strongly insisted upon. For only in this dialectic does the responsibility of faith become clear. He who does not believe is himself guilty. He who believes knows that it is pure grace.

It is impossible to deny this point of contact of divine grace, *i.e.* it is possible to do so only by a misunderstanding. The misunderstanding always arises out of the lack of a distinction between the formal and the material definitions. We said above that materially there is no more *imago Dei*, whereas formally it is intact. Similarly we must say that materially there is no point of contact, whereas formally it is a necessary presupposition. The Word of God does not have to create man's capacity for words. He has never lost it, it is the presupposition of his ability to hear the Word of God. But the Word of God itself creates man's ability to believe the Word of God, *i.e.* the ability to hear it in *such a way* as is only possible in faith. It is evident that the doctrine of *sola gratia* is not in the least endangered by such a doctrine of the point of contact.

The sphere of this "possibility of being addressed" includes not only the *humanum* in the narrower sense, but everything connected with the "natural" knowledge of God. The Word of God could not reach a man who had lost his consciousness of God entirely. A man without conscience cannot be struck by the call "Repent ye and believe the Gospel." What the natural man knows of God, of the law and of his own dependence upon God, may be very confused and distorted. But even so it is the necessary, indispensable point of contact for divine grace. This is also proved by the fact that on the whole the New Testament did not create new words, but uses those that were created by the religious consciousness of the pagans.

(6) This does not mean to say that what the Scriptures say about the death of the old man always refers to the material side of human nature and never to the formal. The subject as such, the fact of self-consciousness, is not destroyed by the act of faith. That is the difference between an act of faith and mystical ecstasy. And this difference points to the personal character of that event, in contrast to the impersonal character of mysticism. The personal God meets man personally. That involves the continuance of self-consciousness. This finds its classical expression in just that passage of the New Testament which approaches most closely to the manner of expression usual in mysticism (Gal. ii. 20): "Nevertheless I live; yet not I, but Christ liveth in me." The phrase "nevertheless I live" follows upon the sentence, "For I through the law am dead. . . . I am crucified with Christ." It means that the formal personality continues beyond the death of the material. But together with this restrictive statement about the formal element we get, as it were by way of correction, an opposite statement concerning the material element: yet not I but *Christ . . . in me.* That is why the New Testament never proceeds to use the expression sometimes used by Luther: that in faith the believer becomes Christ. This formulation is certainly not meant mystically. Nevertheless it is typically mystical and for this reason it is consistently avoided by the New Testament.

The same could be proved about the biblical use of terms concerning the Holy Spirit. The Bible calls faith the work and the gift of the Holy Spirit. Yet it never says: the Holy Spirit within me has faith. But rather:

c

I believe through the Holy Spirit. The passage that comes nearest to the former assertion is 1 Corinthians ii. 10-12. It must surely be interpreted to mean that in so far as we have the Holy Spirit, there takes place in us an act of divine self-consciousness through the Holy Spirit. But it always remains "within us." It never turns into identity. And the conclusion that could be drawn from the analogy of self-consciousness in verse 11 is not drawn. Instead it is turned round: Now we have *received* . . . the things that are *given* to us of God. The identity of the human subject is also guarded where the Spirit is spoken of; therefore the important expression is: to *receive* the Holy Spirit. By holding fast to the identity of the formal personality this expression asserts personal sobriety over against every form of ecstatic exuberance. For this reason also the new creation is never mentioned without the picture of *reparatio*, of restoration, being used at the same time. It is not possible to repair what no longer exists. But it is possible to repair a thing in such a way that one has to say: this has become quite new. Only by means of so sober or careful a manner of expression is it possible to maintain that the act of faith involves personality and decision. And upon this depends the possibility of an imperative of faith, which— as every one knows—is as characteristic of the New Testament as the statement that faith is the gift and work of God. I even think that a statistical survey of New Testament usage would show that the emphasis upon the former is even stronger than upon the latter.

These theses sum up my *theologia naturalis*, of which Karl Barth is so suspicious. There was a time when— like Karl Barth himself—I did not see the contrast between the Gospel and the natural knowledge of God as clearly as I do at present. Anyone who will now read the 1922 edition of Karl Barth's *Epistle to the Romans* will be amazed at the broad stream of platonist speculation about things divine, which has there entered the main stream of biblical theology. The same applies also to my own earlier writings. But I do not think that I should be prepared to take back anything essential of what I said in the first edition of *The Mediator* concerning the natural knowledge of God. I do not wish to deny that I am still of the opinion that there should be an eristic theology based upon this knowledge. But long before I made use of this concept and raised this problem for discussion I realised that it had nothing to do with the question of the "proof of theology." The problem of the proof of theology must be clearly distinguished both from that of eristic theology and also from the closely allied question of "Introduction to Theology" or "formal theology" or "Prolegomena."[14] But I cannot treat of this more fully here.

IV

THE REFORMERS' DOCTRINE AND ITS ANTITHESIS

KARL BARTH has always combined his rejection of my theses with judgments drawn from the history of dogma, which serve him as reasons for his rejection almost every time that he deals with my theses. If it were possible to show that my theses are neither Thomist nor Neo-Protestant but adhere to the teaching of the Reformation, not much would remain of the objections which Barth has so far raised against them. It is not unfair to say that "this is Thomism, that is Neo-Protestantism" is his chief and practically sole argument.

I must admit that I am almost ashamed in under-taking to disprove this. For in this my task is only too

easy. As I cannot at this point write a monograph concerning the *theologia naturalis* of the Reformers, I must be
content to prove the substance of my theses somewhat
from the writings of Calvin. It will be seen that Calvin
goes even further in the direction which Barth calls
"Thomism" or "Neo-Protestantism" than I should
dare to do—though Barth has never stated which
features in this *theologia naturalis* he regards as specifically
Thomist and which specifically Neo-Protestant. Therefore we must formulate our verdict in advance like this:
if Brunner's *theologia naturalis* is Thomist, then this applies
even more to that of Calvin. That this makes it rather
awkward to distinguish between the theology of the
Reformation and that of Thomism should be evident,
especially to those who, in using the word "Reformation," think especially of Calvin. But it would be easy
to show that Luther's views on this subject do not differ
essentially from Calvin's. At some points Luther is more
"Thomist," at others Calvin. In Lutheran "Thomism"
the aristotelian element is somewhat more pronounced,
in Calvinistic "Thomism" the platonic. But the shades
of difference are so fine and the material contained in
the texts of Luther and Calvin shows such great variety
and apparent contradiction that it will be better to
leave such special questions out of account.

To understand Calvin's *theologia naturalis*[15] properly it
is very important to keep in mind the distinction, which
we have already made above, between the *objective* and
the *subjective sense of the word naturalis or natura*. We shall
first treat of *theologia naturalis* in the objective sense, which
is by far the more important.

The word nature, as used by Calvin, means something
quite different from what it does in modern usage. Calvin's
usage is derived from the *linguistic* usage of stoicism—
which dominated the theology of the Church until the
time of the Enlightenment—combined with a charac-

teristic change in *content*. He uses "nature" to designate the original creation[16] in so far as it is still recognisable as such, *i.e.* the God-given form of all created being. This is irrespective of whether it be nature in the modern sense, *i.e.* the world of objects, plants and animals, the human *physis*, or the constant forms in the course of human life, the universal orders of society, or the fundamental laws of cultural and mental life. Nature therefore presents no contrast to spirit or culture, but rather to what is not in accordance with creation, to what has lapsed from the order of creation, to what is arbitrary and irregular.

Therefore nature is for Calvin both a concept of being and a concept of a norm, and over and over again we meet with the expression: *natura docet, natura dictat,* which for him means almost the same as: God teaches— *i.e.* the will of God, which has been implanted in the world from creation, the divine rule of the world, teaches.[17] It is therefore quite natural for Calvin to use the concept of the *lex naturae* and also that of the order of creation in the same sense. Both are used very frequently, but if I am not mistaken *lex naturae* is used more frequently. The will of God, imprinted upon all existence, implanted in it from creation, can therefore be recognised as such.

The divine order of nature—always in the very broad sense, including all things human—is affected by sin not only subjectively—of this later—but also objectively. But it is not affected so much as to render the will of God, the "rule" of nature invisible.[18] On the contrary, where Calvin speaks of nature in the objective sense, he says but little of a disturbance by sin. The more he is concerned with nature apart from man the less does he say, the more he is concerned with man the more does he say. When the centre of the person is under discussion, the personal nucleus, the actual relation to God, then

the two concepts, the objective and the subjective,
coalesce. It is at this point that sin's destructiveness of
creation becomes most evident, or rather it is here
bound together with nature in a personal union, and
therefore the equivocity of the concept of nature—at
one and the same time positive and negative—reaches
its culmination. Calvin can say both: sin is unnatural,
against nature. Or sin is the expression of human nature
in contrast to creation and redemption.[19]

The theological importance of the concept of nature
is shown by the fact that God can be known from nature.[20]
And this is not a confused knowledge, which can hardly
be of interest for the Christian, who knows the Word of
God. On the contrary, it is something highly important
and necessary for the Christian as well. God demands
of us that we should know and honour him in his works.[21]
He has set us into this "theatre"[22] of his glory in order
that in it we should know, contemplate and honour him
as the Lord of glory. God can be known from nature
other than man, but also from man himself. Indeed,
he is to be known especially from the latter. But above
all from *experientia*,[23] *i.e.* from the experience of his
preserving and providential grace. This *experientia* =
knowledge of God is not made superfluous by faith in
the Word of God, but on the contrary remains an important complement of the knowledge of God derived
from Scripture.[24] But the knowledge of God to be gained
from nature is only partial. To put it metaphorically:
from nature we know the hands and feet but not the
heart of God.[25] We can know his wisdom and omni-
potence, also his justice and even his goodness, but not
his forgiving mercy, his absolute will to bring about a
communion between man and himself. But this im-
perfection of the natural knowledge of God is no reason
for underestimating it. Not even he who has been
taught by the Word of God can dispense with it and

is bound to acknowledge it.   Moreover, he is greatly
assisted by it.[26]

The relation of revelation in Scripture to that in
nature is, however, not simple but twofold; through
Scripture the revelation in nature is both clarified and
complemented.   Scripture serves as a "lens",[27] *i.e.* as a
magnifying-glass for natural revelation. Another image:
through the revelation in Scripture the voice of God in
natural revelation is so much amplified that sleeping
man must hear it, whereas otherwise he would fail to
do so.[28]   And secondly, Scripture shows us the heart of
God, which is not revealed in natural revelation—at
least not in its innermost secrets.   But scriptural revelation does not make the natural superfluous.   On the
contrary: only through Scripture is the latter made
effective and only by Scripture are we properly led
to it.[29]

This revelation applies especially also to the knowledge of the divine will from the *law* and the natural
ordinances.   We know the law of God in our reason or
our conscience.   This *lex naturae* is identical in content
with the *lex scripta*, though the *lex scripta* is necessary to
make again perfectly clear the writing of the *lex naturae*
which has, as it were, faded.[30]   But Calvin is concerned
to point out that the *lex scripta* has no other function but
to make the *lex naturae* effective again.   For the *lex
naturae* is the will of God in creation.[31]   The same is true
also of the ordinances.   The ordinances of creation and
nature are also somewhat obscured by sin and need to
be made known again by Christ.   But note: *They* have
to be made known afresh by Christ as ordinances of
creation.[32]   A contemporary theologian has maintained
that a theologian who wants to build his ethics upon the
ordinances of creation and does not become a Roman
Catholic is a dilettante.[33]   If that is so, then Calvin is the
first to whom the verdict applies.   Calvinist ethics are

simply unthinkable without the concept of the ordinances of creation. But before we treat of ethics we have yet to develop a fundamental concept of Calvin's *theologia naturalis*: that of the *imago Dei*, which also forms the transition from *natura* in the objective sense to *natura* in the subjective sense.

The concept of the *imago Dei* is fundamental to Calvinistic anthropology. But in his treatment Calvin makes the inner unity of the whole of his theology appear as clearly as in few other places. This applies above all to the connection of the *theologia naturalis* with the *theologia revelata* in the narrower sense of that term. On the one hand the *imago Dei* points across to christology, since Christ is the original of that likeness,[34] the human *imago*. But it points even more certainly to soteriology since the full content of the *imago Dei* can only be known from the *reparatio*, from the *regeneratio* through Christ and the Holy Spirit.[35] Calvin likes to use the concept *reparatio imaginis* to sum up the whole content of the *regeneratio* which takes place through faith in Christ. These two definitions imply that in a Christian theology the concept of the *imago Dei* can only be understood in conjunction with that of sin as the loss of that *imago*. Apart from man the disturbance or derangement of the *natura*, the order of existence created by God, is, as it were, but a slight one. Consequently the original order clearly shows through the sinful confusion. But here, at the centre of creation, in the case of man, where the personal relation of man and God is at issue, the disturbance is the greatest possible. For here the soul[36] or personal being is human "nature." But the former is as much defined by the concept of sin, *i.e.* of opposition to what is appointed by God, as by the *imago*, that which is appointed by God. This dualism, this inner contradiction in the human essence, is characteristic of man as he is now.[37]

The result of this is the fact that man still and indeed always can and must be spoken of as the image of God. On the other hand, the *imago* must be described as destroyed and spoilt,[38] thoroughly and—apart from the redemption through Christ—irrevocably spoilt. In this Calvin is in total agreement with the hard Augustinian and Lutheran definitions. One should imagine that Calvin was above the suspicion of flirting with Pelagianism.

Nevertheless he avoids falling into the other extreme of saying with Flaccius that original sin is the substance of man or—to say the same in different words—that the *imago Dei* is in no sense a definition of the being of man as he now is. Calvin's explanations amount to more or less what I have called the formal side of the *imago*, without, however, actually employing that term.

Instead of it he uses—like Luther—the concept of a remnant of the *imago*[39] which is somewhat clumsy because of its quantitative appearance. But however quantitative the meaning of the *word*, Calvin's *meaning* and usage are strictly categorical. Calvin considers this remnant of the *imago Dei* to be of great importance. One might almost say that it is one of the pillars supporting his theology. For he identifies it with nothing less than the entire human, rational nature, the immortal soul, the capacity for culture, the conscience, responsibility, the relation with God, which—though not redemptive—exists even in sin, language, the whole of cultural life. And upon it he bases considerable portions of his ethics.[40]

In spite of his sin, man is the most glorious of the creatures of God.[41] In his nature, which is created by God and not entirely destroyed by sin, there continues to manifest itself the will of the Creator, which appointed for man a destiny such as no other creature has. It is this "remnant" of the *imago* which still distinguishes man from the animal and from every other creature and

elevates him above them. Even fallen man still has—
thanks to the "portion" of the *imago* that he has retained
—an immortal soul,[42] a conscience,[43] in which the law of
God is indelibly and irremovably implanted.[44] But he
also has an inclination towards truth and a capacity for
recognising truth. Calvin is not afraid to relate this
lumen naturale directly to the Spirit of God. Especially is
he fond of using in this sense the passage in the prologue
of the fourth Gospel, "the light (of the Logos or of
Christ) shineth in the darkness."[45] Wherever a man of
science investigates the divine laws of the starry heavens,
wherever an artist creates any great works, there the
Spirit of God is active in him, there he is in relation with
divine truth.[46]

Therefore it is not permissible to deprecate or abuse
man. Even in his sin man is yet honourable, since he
still bears the image of God within him, even though it
be obscured and "painted over."[47]

The divine objective and the human subjective factors
show themselves to be different in that the *imago* gives
man occasion to misinterpret himself. One may call to
mind Hamann's famous saying concerning the misunderstanding between reason and itself. The *imago*
gives man occasion for false idealistic speculation, *i.e.* for
an immanentist interpretation of what can be rightly
understood only transcendentally, *i.e.* if the divine act
of creation is taken into consideration.[48] The *imago* is
the seat of responsibility. Similarly it is the seat of
religion, of the knowledge of God and of God's worthiness
to be worshipped. Apropos of these thoughts Calvin
touches upon the distinction between the formal and the
material factors: the *imago* is just sufficient to enable man
to know God but not to know his How, to urge him
towards religion without, however, making a true religion possible for him.[49] Thus also the *imago* is necessary
for any knowledge of God in nature. Here, therefore,

the objective and the subjective concepts meet. The *imago*, which man retains, is the principle of the *theologia naturalis* in the subjective sense, *i.e.* of that knowledge of God derived from nature, of which man is capable apart from revelation in the Scriptures or in Jesus Christ.[50] It is hardly necessary to say that Calvin always treats this *theologia naturalis*, in the subjective sense of *natura*, as a side-issue. For it is of no practical import for us. It has altogether become unnecessary and invalidated through the better knowledge which we have gained in Christ. The subjective natural knowledge of God is not only imperfect but always disfigured by untruth. But in its stead Christ gives us the true *theologia naturalis*, the true knowledge of God in his works in the same way in which he gives us a new knowledge which goes beyond all knowledge that is natural and which is in this sense supernatural.[51]

The interrelation of the two can be seen in the use which Calvin makes of the *imago* in his ethics. *Prima facie* it seems as if Calvin's ethics were based entirely upon the thought of the *imago* still present in sinful man. One might call them purely humanistic ethics. For the object of ethical action is always man or the human community. And this man is—even as a sinner—the image of God. Therefore his life has to be respected. He has the same rights as yourself and you must be just and fair towards him, because he bears the image of God like yourself.[52] Therefore you ought to help him. Especially the idea of the universal relationship of mankind, which is based upon this *imago*, is of importance to Calvin. He who does injury to his neighbour, does injury "to his own flesh." The destruction of the community is the destruction of the body of which we are members.[53] On the one hand Calvin has no scruples in recognising this ethos as one which it is possible within limits for the heathen to achieve as well.[54] (In this matter, as also in his judgment of pagan philosophy, he allows for a variety of degrees.[55]) On the other hand he shows that the sense both of the *imago* and also of this universal relationship can ultimately only be understood in Christ. The true *ethica naturalis*, like the *theologia naturalis*, finds its perfection in Christ alone.[56]

The only thing possible to unregenerate man is a righteousness which amounts exactly to what is otherwise known as *justitia civilis*. It is hardly necessary to say that this righteousness does not count as such before God,[57] though Calvin leaves room for the thought that some few pious men among the heathen might have known the true God and might thus have attained to that righteousness which counts before God.[58] This is possible, because Calvin believes in an original revelation from the time of creation. Its relation to the *lex naturae* is not made clear. But it has never been altogether lost to mankind and has maintained itself especially pure in the case of some few elect.[59]

But let us in conclusion demonstrate the importance of *theologia naturalis* for Calvin by the example of the ordinances. Among the *ordinationes Dei* or *creationis*, matrimony is of special importance to Calvin; among the ordinances of preservation instituted in view of sin, especially the State. All that Calvin says concerning the ethics of matrimony[60] and of the State[61] is derived from his *theologia naturalis*. After what has been said, this means that it is derived from that knowledge of the ordinances of creation which only a Christian can have. The pagan *theologia naturalis* no longer counts. This is to say that Calvin is altogether dependent upon the concept of the *lex naturae* which he derives from creation. This applies at least wherever he is concerned with the problems of the communal life of man, or, as we should say, with social ethics. He is the "dilettante" who bases his ethics upon the ordinances of creation without becoming a

Roman Catholic. It goes without saying that the love which can be rightly understood only through Christ, and which is given by him, is not become invalid. But not even Calvin is prepared to attempt to construct his ethics with that concept alone. The meaning of love in matrimony and in the State has to be seen from the special functions which God has appointed for matrimony and for the State.[62] Both matrimony and the State are instituted by God, though in different senses.[63] Both are under preserving grace and therefore man and his actions are in both instrumental for God.[64] Thus he likes to call those responsible for the State the "lieutenants" or "officers" of God.[65] He even goes so far as to see proof of the divine dignity of the State in the fact that the Scriptures call its officers "gods."[66] Only so can it be understood how Calvin is able to see the two ordinances, the State an ordinance of preservation and the Church an ordinance of redemption, together in one unity in Christ and yet assigns to each not only a totally different function but a totally different law.[67]

This is, roughly speaking, Calvin's *theologia naturalis*. In all essentials it is also that of Luther.[68] There can be no question as to whether this is the doctrine of the Reformation but merely whether at this point there is any difference between the Roman Catholic Thomist doctrine and that of the Reformers. In no case can the difference be where Barth sees it; for Barth considers the characteristic of the Reformers' theology to be the denial of the *theologia naturalis*. But there is a difference, and even a very considerable one, only it is at quite a different point. After what has been said we can summarise this difference as follows: in Roman Catholicism the objective and the subjective concepts of nature coalesce, they coincide, as it were, completely. The reason for this is the doctrine of the *imago Dei*.

According to Roman Catholic doctrine man has not

lost the *imago* through sin at all, but only the *dona superaddita*, the *justitia*—or, more properly, the *perfectio— originalis*. Sin has, as it were, nothing to do with this question. This means that there is an *unrefracted theologia naturalis*. There is a *system* of natural theology, a self-sufficient rational system, detachable from *theologia revelata* and capable of serving it for a solid foundation. That is the great contrast to the theology of the Re-formers. Thanks to the undamaged *imago* the *theologia naturalis* is derivable from reason alone. It is purely rational and as such complete. There is such a thing as rational theology and therefore also rational ethics or moral philosophy is possible. Nature, *i.e.* the divine order of creation, is entirely accessible and adequately intelligible to reason, since the two concepts of nature, the objective and the subjective, coincide completely. Reason is competent and adequate in dealing with "nature." Only supernature, that which bears upon redemption, is reserved for faith.[69]

Thus the natural knowledge of God is freed from the twilight that lies upon it in the doctrine of the Reformers. There is no antinomy in it. A dichotomy has taken the place of the antinomy. On the one hand nature, on the other grace, on the one hand reason, on the other revelation. Both are neatly divided by a horizontal line, distinguished from one another like the first and second storeys of a building. For the Reformers no statement concerning nature can be quite correct unless Christ be taken into account. Even in matters of natural revelation the *lumen naturale* is sufficient only up to a certain degree, which is never capable of being accurately fixed. But in Roman Catholicism the *lumen naturale* is co-extensive with nature itself. Or, to put it differently: the *theologia naturalis* is for the Reformers dialectical, for Roman Catholicism undialectical. The Reformers did not pay much attention to this question. Their interest in this matter was concentrated upon one point: *justitia*, free will, the intactness of human reason in questions of ethics and religion. The idea that the *imago Dei* in man is intact provokes their wrath. They follow up the consequences of this idea and of its opposite, as it were, only upwards, in the direction of soteriology but not downwards, in the direction of *theologia naturalis*. This is why hardly one Protestant theologian is properly informed on this subject.

But the fault of this lies above all in the fact that the concept of nature, which was common to all theology until the time of the Enlightenment, had been lost and was therefore not understood by the theologians of the nineteenth century who went back to the Reformers.[70] It need hardly be said that the concept of nature which gained currency at the time of the Enlightenment was completely different both from that of Catholicism and from that of the Reformers. If one wanted to put it metaphorically, one would have to say that for the Reformers the light of the revelation in Christ must shine into nature in order to light up this foundation. The Roman Catholics separate them by a neat horizontal line. For the Enlightenment the light of reason reaches upwards into the sphere of redemption to the extent of doing away completely with the distinction between the *lumen naturale* and the revelation in Christ. The *lumen naturale* now becomes itself a revelation, indeed the only one that there really is. Thus the whole of theology becomes *theologia naturalis*, or at least the distinction between the revelation in Christ or in the Scriptures and rational knowledge becomes blurred and uncertain. Rationalism proper is the complete abolition of the distinction. But what Barth means by Neo-Protestantism is this confused mixture of both principles. In the Reformers' theology the independence of the natural knowledge of God is, as it were, rightly threatened by revelation. But here, on the contrary, the independence

of revelation is threatened by rational knowledge. Roman
Catholicism, with its neat line of demarcation between
reason and revelation, stands in the middle.

As regards the controversy between Barth and myself,
the picture would have to be completed thus: in Barth's
theology *theologia naturalis* is not only threatened and
restricted by revelation but it is altogether done away
with. My theses aim at strengthening the movement of
the Reformers, which diverges from the Roman Catholic
horizontal line, without going beyond it—or, in terms of
our metaphor, below it—as does Barth's complete denial.
Therefore my theology can be accused as an "approxi-
mation to Roman Catholicism" from Barth's point of
view but not from that of the Reformers' teaching.

It is possible to agree to some extent with this proof
from the history of dogma, as Barth has done recently,[71]
and to maintain that the Reformers' doctrine of the *lex
naturae* and natural theology is obscure and not clearly
thought out and that they failed to assert the contrast
with sufficient sharpness. If that is so, then it is hardly
right to characterise those that hold the doctrine of the
Reformers rather than that of Barth, as Thomistic and
opposed to the Reformation, though they may objectively
be wrong in so doing. But the Reformers' teaching on
this point is perfectly clear and consistent, though it may
not be thought out so thoroughly as at other points. Nor
is it objectively wrong. That has been discussed in
section III.

We may ask why Barth should so violently and
brusquely deny a doctrine which is obviously in accordance with the Scriptures and the Reformation, in spite
of his being otherwise so loyal to Scripture and being so
seriously concerned to recapture the message of the
Reformation. I believe that the answer lies in a one-sided
concept of revelation. Barth refuses to recognise that
where revelation and faith are concerned, there can be

anything permanent, fixed, and, as it were, natural. He acknowledges only the act, the event of revelation, but never anything revealed, or, as he says, the fact of revelation. The whole strength of Barthian theology lies in the assertion of the actual. It is here that revelation in the ultimate, fullest sense can only be an act, God speaking to me here and now. But that is only one side of the biblical concept of revelation. The other side is its very opposite. It is the fact that God speaks to me here and now because he *has* spoken. Above all, that he speaks to me through the Holy Spirit because he has spoken in Jesus Christ. This "has" is maintained in the concept of the Canon. The Bible is the "fact of the revelation" of God. It is true that the Scriptures become the Word of God for me only through the Holy Spirit. But *they* become the Word of God for me and they become it because they already *are* it. They become it through *that, which* is written, the solid body of words, sentences and books, something objective and available for every one. If I may use this trivial comparison, the relation of the Bible to the actual revelation of God is like that of the gramophone record to the sounding music, which has been engraved upon it and is again taken out of it. It is a "record," an action become substance. It is fixed and unalterable. It is a piece of world at anyone's disposal, even though the fact of its being a revelation is not at anyone's disposal. That which is at anyone's disposal, this Book of books with its fixed text, is what God uses in order to speak his personal Word to me to-day. That is his will. Only through that which is fixed and given does he will to give me his direct personal Word.

Once we have understood this, it is not difficult to acknowledge the fact that God speaks to us through his work in nature, in the wide sense of the old usage. The whole arrangement of the world, with its fixity and the permanency of its being, is a manifestation of God. It

D

does not bear this function "in itself"—any more than the Scriptures—but only because to this Word is added an ear that hears it, to this manifestation an eye that sees it. This expression of God is also subject to the subject-object correlation. An expression is only an expression where there is an impression to correspond to it. It is impossible to see the expression of God without it making an impression. Where that is so, the Scriptures speak of sin and unbelief both where natural revelation is concerned and also where scriptural revelation (or prophetic revelation or revelation in Christ) is concerned. God does not speak to us except by signs and pictures. By the picture-language of the order of the world and by that of the prophetic and apostolic word. Even Jesus Christ is a piece of picture-language or, as Kierkegaard puts it, an "indirect communication." For direct communication is paganism. Direct communication cannot communicate the message of God, but only that of an idol. That is the reason why it is not possible to deny the "fact of revelation" of God in the order of the world or of nature for the reasons which Barth gives, *e.g.* in the context of his rejection of the *analogia entis*. For if one did so, one would also have to abandon the fact of the revelation of God in Scripture, and would thus lapse into an enthusiastic idea of revelation. But this parallel with Scripture does not by any means exhaustively show the significance of natural revelation and therefore of *theologia naturalis* for the Church and for theology.

V

THE SIGNIFICANCE OF *THEOLOGIA NATURALIS* FOR THEOLOGY AND THE CHURCH

SOME years ago I had a discussion with Karl Barth concerning *theologia naturalis* which I shall not easily forget. In it he pointed out to me the political danger of Gogarten's doctrine of the ordinances. His verdict was that in that concept there was hidden a whole political and cultural programme of a distinctly authoritarian stamp. Events have proved how right he was. Even then —long before the publication of my book, *The Divine Imperative* (E.T.)—I tried to show that there are two possible ways of conceiving of orders. One of these is strictly conservative and authoritarian. The other, which might be called revolutionary or conservative with equal justification, is a "refracted" concept of orders, corresponding to the refraction in the *theologia naturalis* of the Reformers. But Barth was then as little interested in this distinction as he is now.

That much is clear: the theologian's attitude to *theologia naturalis* decides the character of his ethics. Historically it may be said that the concept of the ordinances of creation has been regulative for Christian ethics from the beginning to the time of the Enlightenment, in all matters connected with the problem of society as such, *i.e.* in the doctrines of the ministry, secular vocation, matrimony, the State, etc. Christian social ethics throughout the centuries may be defined as the doctrine of the love founded in Jesus Christ and of its function in society *according to the divine institution of the latter*. Social ethics are therefore always determined as much by the concept of the divine grace of creation and preservation as by that of the redeeming grace of Christ. The point at issue between the primitive and reformed doctrine on the one hand and the Roman Catholic and Thomist doctrine on the other is not *whether* the idea of the ordinances of creation and preservation should determine the behaviour of Christians, but *how* it should do so. Only the individualism and the rationalism of the Enlightenment destroyed the appreciation of this central idea and the nineteenth century regained it only in some rare instances, even where theologians were determined to return to the Bible and the Reformation.[72]

The result of this abandonment is an invincible individualism. All attempts to operate with the concepts of love or with those of "law" or "commandment" without the help of the concept of the ordinances, lead either to rationalistic social constructions (liberalistic doctrines of the State and matrimony) or to an uncertain attitude towards the ordinances of society as given factors, vacillating between acknowledgment and rejection. But we have to acknowledge the fact that God has not simply put us into a "world," but into his creation, whose laws can be known in spite of sin, by those who know God in Jesus Christ. This means that we have to acknowledge divinely appointed objective limits to our freedom and objective guides to the ordering of our society. That is the only way out of this chaos—the way which gives to the Reformers' ethics on the one hand their assurance, and on the other hand their realism. Luther's distinction between office and person, his entire doctrine of vocation and status, is informed by the idea of preserving grace and of the ordinances of creation and preservation which are its instruments. The same is true of his clear distinction between Church and State.[73] All those who—quite irrespective of their motives—act in accordance with the laws of these ordinances, do the works of God. They are not thereby justified before God—that can happen only by faith, *i.e.* by doing these works in the knowledge of divine grace, in obedience to and confidence in God—but they do "right."

In so doing they can claim that they have fulfilled civil justice, without thereby being justified in the sight of God. The same applies to all those who fulfil the law of God—whether the written or the *lex naturae*—in any way whatsoever. The ordinances—*e.g.* the ordinance of matrimony, *i.e.* the demand that man should live in monogamous marriage, and the ordinance of the State, *i.e.* the obedient acknowledgment of civil authority— are a part of the divine law. The law—whether it be written law or the *lex naturae* or one of these ordinances— is the form in which the divine will is revealed, which only through the Holy Spirit becomes a concrete divine commandment, governing my existence here and now. Only the Holy Spirit teaches us to know the law and the ordinances truly, in accordance with the needs of the moment. Moreover, he alone gives the strength to obey them in such a way that the will of God is done not only outwardly but inwardly also. It would yet have to be seen what a system of biblical or reformed ethics would look like which dispensed with this central doctrine as taught by the Reformers. I, for one, would not be prepared to prophesy any success for such an experiment.

But *theologia naturalis*, in the sense in which I have defined it, is significant not only for ethics but for dogmatics also. This is the place for a few words concerning the principle of analogy and Barth's polemic against it. Barth is the first theologian to see in the use of the principle of analogy a—or even *the*—contrast between Protestantism and Roman Catholicism. For Barth holds the strange doctrine that there is no creature which has in itself any likeness to God. Rather is it raised to this status by the revelation in Christ and through the Holy

Spirit.[74] This is a piece of theological nominalism, in comparison with which that of William of Occam appears harmless. For this would mean that we call God "Father," "Son," "Spirit," that we speak of the "Word" of God, etc., not because God is more like a father than anything else, but simply because God says so in the Scriptures. God does not say it because by his creation and from his creation it is so, but, on the contrary, it only becomes so by the Word of God in Scripture.

In fact and in truth Barth is not able to maintain this extreme nominalism consistently. Barth's *Dogmatics*, like all others, are of course based on the idea of analogy, even though he does not acknowledge this. The passage where this becomes visible is the one in which he says the following concerning the Word of God: The form in which reason communicates with reason, person with person, is language, so, too, when it is God's language. Of course it is divine reason that communicates with human reason, the divine person with the human person. The complete inconceivability of this event confronts us. *But reason with reason, person with person, primarily in analogy with what happens in the spiritual sphere of creation, not primarily in analogy with what happens in the corporal or natural sphere.* The Word of God is a rational and not an irrational event. (*Dogmatics*, E.T., p. 152 ff.) But this means that at least at this point the principle of analogy is used in the sense in which Barth otherwise rejects it: Human reason is in itself—*i.e.* by divine creation—more suitable for a definition of the nature of God than stocks or stones. And in the same way the word is in itself—*i.e.* by divine creation—a suitable means of establishing relations between two subjects, not only between man and man but also between God and man. The fact that man is a subject is in itself analogous to the fact that God is a subject. Hence we must exclude all other analogies

and make the fact that God is a subject the governing
thought in our theology—as Barth quite rightly does.
But this means that the whole Barthian theology rests
de facto upon the doctrine of the formal *imago Dei*, which
he so much dislikes, *i.e.* upon the doctrine that man as
we know him, sinful man, is the only legitimate analogy
to God, because he is always a rational being, a subject,
a person. To put it differently: man's nature as *imago Dei*
determines that he should not speak of God except by
way of human metaphor. Father, Son, Spirit, Word—
these all-important concepts of Christian theology, of
the message of the Bible, are concepts derived from
personality. They are not set apart for this purpose
from all concepts derived from nature (in the modern
sense of the word), because God—incomprehensibly—
wants it to be so, but rather because in man God has
created a being like to himself, the only being like to
himself, whose likeness to him (*i.e.* the fact that he is a
subject and a person) is not destroyed even by sin.
Consequently his likeness is, in contrast to all analogies
from nature, confirmed by revelation. Thus without
knowing it and without wishing it, Barth himself argues
in favour of *theologia naturalis* and of its fundamental
significance in theology. In the same way he contradicts
by his theology his programme "Against the *analogia
entis!*" The *analogia entis* is not specifically Roman
Catholic. Rather is it the basis of every theology, of
Christian theology as much as of pagan. The characteristic of Christian theology, and somehow also the difference between Roman Catholic and Protestant theology,
is not the issue *whether* the method of analogy may be
used, but *how* this is to be done and *what* analogies are
to be employed. The determining factor in Christian
theology is the energy with which the fact that God is a
subject is—in contrast to other analogies—maintained in
theology. This determining factor rests upon the doctrine

of the *imago Dei*, which can be adequately understood only in the incarnation of God.

Let me also point out briefly the practical ecclesiastical significance of *theologia naturalis*. The task of the Church is the proclamation of her message. The Church can effect this proclamation in various ways—by preaching, by teaching, by pastoral work, by theology, by personal witness, etc. But wherever the Church proclaims the Word of God in human words, she must choose from amongst human words those that somehow correspond adequately to the divine Word. The objective reason for this correspondence, *i.e.* for the possibility of speaking of God and of proclaiming his Word at all, is the fact that God has made us in his image. The subjective reason is the revelation of this fact made to us in Jesus Christ. The incarnation is the *criterion of the knowledge* of the divine likeness of man, of its truth and of its profundity. But man's undestroyed formal likeness to God is the *objective possibility* of the revelation of God in his "Word."

The Church could not proclaim her message but for the creaturely relation between the word of man and the Word of God. The fact of the Church's message rests upon this "remnant" of the *imago Dei*. The contents of this message rest upon the restoration of the image in Christ. The Church also is dependent upon the possibility "of speaking to man of God at all." That is the "point of contact": capacity for words and responsibility. But the effectiveness of the Church's proclamation does not rest on this general possibility alone, but also upon whether this contact is made in the right way or the wrong way. The Church's proclamation must be *comprehensible* else it is useless, however true its contents. The Holy Ghost alone can open man's heart for the Word of God, so that he can understand and accept it. This must not make us indifferent towards the contents of our human words in which we proclaim the Word of

God. We believe that there is a close relation between our pure doctrine and the activity of the Holy Spirit. But neither must it make us indifferent towards the form of our proclamation.

No less a man than Luther, the protagonist of the objective Word of God, related the attention to be paid to the manner of our proclamation with the core of the contents of our preaching, with the doctrine of the incarnation of the Son of God. In the place in the "German Mass," where he gives simple rules for the Christian instruction of children, he continues: "And let no one think himself too wise and despise such child's play. When Christ was desirous of instructing men, he must needs become a man. If we wish to instruct children (viz. in Christ) we must needs become children with them. I wish to God such child's play were well played. We should soon see great treasure come from Christian men and perceive souls grow rich in Holy Writ and in the knowledge of God. . . ." Grown-ups also should use such pedagogic helps for themselves, "else they will go daily to hear a sermon and come thence as they have gone. For they think that they need do nothing but pass time in hearing it, neither do they propose to profit therefrom or to keep it. Upon this wise not a few hear sermons for three or four years, yet do they not learn enough that they might give account of any part of the creed. It is true there is enough of it written in books. Nevertheless it is not yet written into the hearts." (*Vide* Weimar Edition, XIX, 78.)

A true appreciation of *theologia naturalis* and of its relation to the revelation in Christ is a presupposition for all kinds of Christian education both in the widest and in the narrowest sense of the word, *i.e.* for every knowledge of the right method of proclamation in relation to the right substance. Experience teaches that wherever *theologia naturalis* is despised, there also the pedagogic factor is despised—which necessarily has disastrous consequences in the Church. We are certainly not concerned here with a question of "mere psychology." *What* I should say to a man upon his death-bed is a holy matter; but it is a matter no less holy how I am to say it to him in such a way that he shall understand and appreciate it. A pastor might—to put it somewhat strongly—go to heaven on account of the What but go to hell on account of the How. To despise the question of the How is a sign, not of theological seriousness but of theological intellectualism. The What is, as it were, guarded by faith, but the How has to be guarded by love. But where the How and therefore love is lacking, there faith must be lacking also.

But *theologia naturalis* is also of decisive importance for the dealings of Christians with unbelievers. At this point there is a danger of the true principles being betrayed. As early as the second century the Apologists did this, and since then it has happened again and again. But the task remains. The fact that there is a false apologetic way of making contact does not mean that there is not a right way. The wrong way of making contact is, to put it briefly, to prove the existence of God. For this pre-supposes the Roman Catholic view of *theologia naturalis*, a self-sufficient rational system of natural knowledge of God. But though proof is excluded, this does not exclude the possibility of a discussion pointing towards such evidence of the existence of God as we have. The decisive factor will always be the simple proclamation of the Christian message. But there is such a thing as theological work done upon the message, *i.e.* intellectual work in the realm of concepts, which can and is intended to serve the proclamation of the message. Similarly there is such a thing as an intellectual and conceptual work of preparation, which clears obstacles out of the way of proclamation. Every one who carries on pastoral work among intellectuals or has the task of instructing modern youth, knows the significance of this. But the centre on which everything turns is the centre of the *theologia naturalis*: the doctrine of the *imago Dei* and especially of responsibility. The explication of the concept of responsibility is the subject-matter of theological eristics. It can easily be seen from what Calvin says concerning this subject how far this is possible by way of *theologia naturalis*. But complete isolation would soon—and nowadays more so than ever—result in the Church despising all *theologia naturalis*. What is central is not dogmatics, nor eristics, nor ethics, but solely the proclamation of the Word of God itself. But a true understanding of *theologia naturalis* is of decisive importance for all three and also for the manner of proclamation.

I do not wish to blame Karl Barth for neglecting and discrediting *theologia naturalis*. God uses the genius of one-sidedness—which is perhaps a pleonasm—as much as the spirits of moderation. He made use of Luther's one-sidedness, monstrous though it was at some points, as much as the comprehensive and balanced thought of Calvin. It may be Barth's special mission to serve at this point as a counter-weight to dangerous aberrations. There really can be no difference of opinion between us that a false natural theology did great damage to the Protestantism of the last century—or should we say of the last three centuries? And a false theology derived from nature is also at the present time threatening the Church to the point of death. No one has taught us as clearly as Karl Barth that we must here fight with all the passion, strength and circumspection that we can muster. But the Church must not be thrown from one extreme to the other. In the long run the Church can bear the rejection of *theologia naturalis* as little as its misuse. It is the task of our theological generation to find the way back to a true *theologia naturalis*. And I am convinced that it is to be found far away from Barth's negation and quite near Calvin's doctrine. If we had enquired from the master earlier, this dispute amongst us disciples would not have arisen. It is high time to wake up for the opportunity that we have missed.

FOOTNOTES

[1] This was already clearly apparent in the essays, "Das erste Gebot als theologisches Axiom," *Zwischen den Zeiten*, 1933, p. 311 ff., and somewhat less bluntly in the preface to the English edition of the *Epistle to the Romans*, and in the *Church Dogmatics*, p. 27 ff.

[2] *Zwischen den Zeiten*, last issue identical with *Theologische Existenz heute*, No. 7, p. 33.

[3] I must here, as I have done in my "Ethik," call to mind the forgotten though most important representative of a truly Lutheran theology in the nineteenth century, A. von Oettingen and his *Lutherische Dogmatik* in three volumes. This distinguishes itself from the Lutheranism of Erlangen by its complete freedom from the influence of Schleiermacher and from that of Saxony and Prussia by its very much greater flexibility. But I must also reckon Kaehler among the truly biblical theologians who did much to prepare the way for the dialectical theology. As regards the question here at issue, my position is nearer to Kaehler than to Schlatter. Altogether Kaehler has anticipated most of the questions which occupy us nowadays.

[4] In the essay concerning the first commandment, which I have already mentioned, Barth makes his polemic against me—and also against Gogarten and Bultmann—easy by taking the phrase "and reason" to mean a second source of theological knowledge independent of biblical revelation. The basic thought of my book is, as will be shown below, that only through Jesus or Holy Scripture do we properly understand these ordinances which are given by God and thus understand them to be the divine rule for our activity in society ("in office and calling"). These divine ordinances also make life possible for the heathen who, however, do not recognize their origin or their meaning clearly.

[5] E.T.: *The Divine Imperative* (Tr.).

[6] Compare my essay "Theologie und Kirche," *Zwischen den Zeiten*, 1930, p. 397 ff.

[7] His polemic has become more and more pronounced since his lecture "Zur Lehre vom Heiligen Geist" (E.T.: "The Holy Ghost and the Christian Life"). Important above all is what he says in the *Church Dogmatics*, the essay on the first commandment, and the latest "Gottes Wille und unsere Wüensche," *Theologische Existenz heute*, No. 7.

[8] Schumann's essay: "*Imago Dei*" in the volume of collected essays of the theologians of Giessen (under the same title; pub. 1932), shows the struggle

of "Old Lutheran" theology with the two senses of the doctrine of the *imago*. Schumann rightly says there that the doctrine of the remnant of the *imago* "does not derive in any way from a semi-Pelagian dilution of the doctrine of original sin," but "from a genuine and original dogmatic necessity." Schumann's solution, however, does not seem to me to be satisfactory.

⁹ The reason why Barth has nowhere dealt with the important passages Romans i. and ii.—for he himself would surely agree that the relevant passages in his *Epistle to the Romans* do not count in this connection—is no doubt that Barth simply refuses to follow St. Paul here, and in addition regards these passages as an *hapax legomenon*. But in reality they are a clear reminder that St. Paul always presupposes the Old Testament and with it its manifold witness to the glory of God as Creator which finds expression in his works.

¹⁰ As far as I know, Barth has nowhere discussed the question what, according to his view, is the theological significance of the general human ethical consciousness, the consciousness of responsibility towards a holy law or a holy will. For Luther the significance is quite clear: *habent cognitionem legalem*. The fact that the *cognitio legalis* is not saving knowledge of God never means for Luther that it is no knowledge of God at all. The contrary is clearly to be seen from hundreds of passages. On this depends the whole dialectic of Luther's theology; compare the excellent discussion in Th. Harnack: *Luthers Theologie*, Vol. I, especially chapters 10 and 11.

¹¹ It is not permissible to abolish the duality of the revelation of God in creation and in Jesus Christ by saying that creation is only known in Christ —as Barth has often done since writing his work on the Holy Spirit. Rather do we know through Jesus Christ that God has revealed himself to us before, but that we did not properly admit this revelation: cf. what I have said below concerning Calvin. Actually Barth knows this too. On p. 508 of the *Church Dogmatics* (E.T.) he says that the Word of Christ is none other than that by which we also were created. "The same Jesus Christ through whom God binds us to himself while yet enemies, the same has already bound himself to us, as those who belong to him, because he alone has called us out of nothingness. And by this our *first* bond with him, as it becomes manifest to us in the second and through the second, through his revelation is measured the meaning which this *second* bond itself must have for us." Barth is right in deducing responsibility from this. Barth therefore agrees with the Epistle to the Hebrews that the Word of Christ as the Word of creation upholds and preserves us all. This means that objectively we somehow live by the Word of God even as sinners. But Barth rejects the idea that God in any way *testifies* to himself as creator outside the revelation in Jesus Christ. In this respect his doctrine departs as much from the Bible as it does from the Reformation. He acknowledges here only a general *grace*, but not a corresponding general *revelation*.

¹² Cf. Acts xiv. 17.

¹³ There is also a type of human activity within the sphere of redeeming grace. We call it the activity of the Church.

¹⁴ Barth's misunderstanding (*Church Dogmatics* (E.T.), p. 28) that what I mean by eristic theology is a *foundation* of theology is no doubt due to the fact that in my essay "Die andere Aufgabe der Theologie" ("The other

task of Theology"), *Zwischen den Zeiten*, 1929, p. 273, I assign to it a *preparatory* function. Such theological work can indeed be a preparation for the hearing of the Word of God.

[15] In the following paragraphs I owe many references and some new pieces of insight into the ramifications of Calvin's *theologia naturalis* to the (as yet unprinted) work of my pupil, G. Gloede, *Theologia Naturalis bei Calvin*. In it he has collected an enormous number of references from the complete works of the Genevan Reformer and has impressively set out Calvin's natural theology in relation to his doctrine of creation and revelation. The references are all to the *Corpus Reformatorum*. (The work referred to above has since appeared in the *Tübinger Studien zur systematischen Theologie*, Stuttgart, 1935—Tr.)

[16] Vol. XLVII, p. 5, line 2; Vol. XXXVIII, p. 77, line 11.

[17] Vol. XXIV, p. 657, line 48*; p. 662, line 44; Vol. XXIII, p. 51, line 12*; p. 368, line 8.

[18] Vol. XXIV, p. 603, line 31; Vol. XXIII, p. 141, line 39.

[19] Vol. XXIII, p. 141, line 39; Vol. II, p. 212, line 55.

[20] Vol. XXIII, pp. 11-12; Vol. XLV, p. 182, line 32; Vol. XLVII, p. 7, line 3; Vol XXXIII, p. 572, line 24*; Vol XXXI, p. 88, line 6; p. 91, line 3.*

[21] Vol. II, p. 47, line 48*; Vol. XXIII, pp. 9-10; Vol. XLVIII, p. 328, line 42; Vol. XLVII, p. 59, line 7; Vol. XXIII, p. 23, line 40.

[22] Vol. XXIII, p. 11, line 12; Vol. XLVIII, p. 328, line 42; Vol. XXIII, p. 9, line 18*; Vol. II, p. 47, line 11.*

[23] Vol. XXXI, p. 88, line 6; Vol. II, p. 43, line 44; Vol. XLIX, p. 340, line 37*; Vol. XLVII, p. 5, line 29.*

[24] Vol. XXIII, p. 584, line 24; p. 210, line 41; p. 584, line 24.*

[25] Vol. XXIII, p. 11, line 4.

[26] Vol. XLIX, p. 326, line 1, and No. 3.

[27] Vol. XXIII, pp. 9-10; Vol. II, p. 53, line 27.*

[28] Vol. XXXIII, p. 604, line 13.

[29] Vol. XXXIII, p. 423, line 31; Vol. XLIX, p. 326, line 1; Vol. II, p. 267, line 23*; Vol. XXIV, p. 627, line 23.*

[30] Vol. II, p. 267, line 5; Vol. I, p. 29, line 18.

[31] Vol. I, p. 29, line 1; Vol. X, p. 236, line 40*; Vol. XXXII, p. 86, line 54.*

[32] Vol. XLVII, p. 7, line 10; p. 5, line 7*; Vol. XXXVIII, p. 77, line 11.*

[33] Froer, *Was ist evangelische Erziehung?* 1933, p. 12.

[34] Vol. XXIII, pp. 11-12.

[35] Vol. XXIII, p. 26, line 41.

[36] Vol. XXIII, p. 27, line 5; Vol. LV, p. 411, line 32.

[37] Vol. II, p. 176, line 11; Vol. XXIII, p. 118, line 29; Vol. II, p. 195, line 55; Vol. XLVII, p. 57, line 38.

[38] Vol. XXIII, p. 52, line 42; Vol. II, p. 179, line 44; p. 138, line 27.

[39] Vol. XXXI, p. 92, line 20*; Vol. XXVIII, p. 488, line 52*; Vol. XLVII, p. 57, line 33*; Vol. XXIII, p. 26, line 38.*

[40] Vol. XXXI, p. 92, line 20; Vol. XXIII, p. 100, line 3; Vol. XXXV, p. 74, line 42*; Vol. XXVI, p. 438, line 35.*

[41] Vol. XXXIII, p. 662, line 16; Vol. VIII, p. 348, line 22; Vol. XXVI, p. 255, line 44; Vol. II, p. 149, line 26; Vol. XXXI, p. 94, line 11; and 33; Vol. II, p. 133, line 29.

[42] Vol. XLIX, p. 558, line 17; Vol. VII, p. 112, line 24.

[43] Vol. XXIV, p. 662, line 44*; Vol. XLIX, p. 129, line 48; Vol. II, p. 267, line 5*; Vol. I, p. 29, line 18.*

[44] Vol. XXIV, p. 725, line 7; Vol. XLIX, p. 38, line 10; Vol. XXIII, p. 431, line 24.

[45] Vol. XLIX, p. 344, line 44; Vol. XLVII, p. 7, line 10*; Vol. XXIII, p. 39, line 1*; Vol. XXXIII, p. 489, line 41*; Vol. II, p. 198, line 32.

[46] Vol. XXXVIII, p. 59, line 5; Vol. XXXIII, p. 422, line 32.

[47] Vol. II, p. 196, line 7*; Vol. LV, p. 411, line 36.

[48] Vol. XXIII, p. 39, line 40*; Vol. II, p. 43, line 48; Vol. II, p. 196, line 29.*

[49] Vol. XLIX, p. 38, line 35; Vol. LI, p. 204, line 52.*

[50] Vol. V, p. 180, line 42*; Vol. XLIX, p. 326, line 1.

[51] Vol. XLVII, p. 7, line 3; Vol. XXIII, p. 26, line 38.

[52] Vol. XXII, pp. 42-43.

[53] Vol. XXVI, p. 304, line 19*; Vol. XXV, p. 180, line 16*; Vol. XXIII, p. 488, line 44.

[54] Vol. XXIII, p. 291, line 23; Vol. XXIV, p. 679, line 32.

[55] Vol. XXIII, p. 46, line 21*; p. 85, line 22*; Vol. II, p. 49, line 30*; p. 38, line 12.*

[56] Vol. XLIX, p. 53, line 43; p. 477, line 46.

[57] Vol. II, p. 212, line 31.

[58] Vol. XXXIII, p. 27, line 6; Vol. XXV, p. 266, line 31.

[59] Vol. XXIV, p. 30, line 39*; Vol. XLIX, pp. 207-208; Vol. XXV, p. 267, line 45*; p. 277, line 24.*

[60] Vol. XLV, p. 528, line 29; Vol. XXIII, p. 99, line 32*; Vol. XLIX, p. 410, line 11.*

[61] Vol. XLIX, p. 249, line 36; Vol. LIII, p. 143, line 43; Vol. LV, p. 245, line 10; Vol. XXIV, p. 354, line 47.

[62] Vol. XLIX, p. 122, line 20*; p. 474, line 17; Vol. XXIII, p. 50, line 38.*

[63] Vol. XXIII, p. 49, line 37.

[64] Vol. XLIX, p. 187, line 54; Vol. XXIII, p. 44, line 32.*

[65] Vol. XXIV, p. 187, line 25; Vol. LIII, p. 138, line 44.

[66] Vol. VII, p. 83, line 22.

[67] Vol. LIII, p. 137, line 13; Vol. VII, p. 89, line 1; Vol. XLVII, p. 7, line 3*; Vol. VII, p. 89, line 1.*

[68] Cf. Lau, "*Ausserliche Ordnung*" *und* "*Weltlich Ding*" *in Luthers Theologie* ("External Order" and "Worldly Matter" in the theology of Luther), 1933. Protestant theologians frequently maintain that Luther did not acknowledge any rule of natural law concerning matrimony, the State,

the Law, etc. But this assertion rests upon the equation of natural law with its Thomist interpretation. According to Luther society is regulated *only* by natural law. But the application of this law of nature is historically variable. There is no *a priori* or rigid subjection to natural law.

⁶⁹ Cf. my excursus concerning Roman Catholic natural law in *The Divine Imperative* (E.T.), p. 627.

⁷⁰ Thus also the discussion between Holl and Troeltsch suffers from this lack of understanding of the universal ecclesiastical concept of the *lex naturae* and its modification through Luther. The same is true—in contrast to the above-mentioned work of Lau—of H. Steubing's monograph, *Naturrecht und natürliche Theologie im Protestantismus* (Natural law and Natural Theology in Protestantism), 1932.

⁷¹ *Theologische Existenz heute*, No. 7, p. 25, and similarly in his Barmen-lecture.

⁷² Lutherans like von Oettingen and Vilmar, whom not even Barth would dare to reckon among the "Neo-Protestants," have brought out the significance of the ordinances of creation in their ethics. The same is true of such Dutch Calvinists as Kuyper and Bavink.

⁷³ Luther's doctrine on this topic is certainly "unequivocal" (Barth): "The government of the world is full well appointed by God, so that it was not needful that God should send down his beloved Son into our miserable flesh into the world so that he might shed his blood for the bodily and worldly governing thereof. For that very same law was before established through those in the estate of matrimony and through the government of the State" (*vide* Luther's works, Weimar Edition, Vol. XLVII, p. 242). Luther's whole social ethics are based on that "Word of God" of which Luther said: "Ideo enimD eus *nobiscum loquitur* et agit *per . . . parentes, per magistratus . . .* sive sum pater, sive mater, sive filius, audio verbum . . . *Deus enim mecum loquitur in ipso statu vitae in quo vivo*" (Weimar Edition, Vol. XLIII, p. 478). For a description of the manner in which this idea runs through Luther's whole social ethics and forms their basis, cf. Lau, *op. cit.*

⁷⁴ Barth, *Church Dogmatics* (E.T.), pp. 134 f., 274 f., 383 f.

KARL BARTH

NO!

Answer to Emil Brunner

E

PREFACE

I AM by nature a gentle being and entirely averse to all unnecessary disputes. If anyone, faced with the fact that he is here reading a controversial treatise, should suggest that it would be so much nicer if theologians dwelt together in unity, he may rest assured that I heartily agree with him. Let me also impress upon him that, humanly and personally speaking, I have nothing against Emil Brunner. On the contrary I greatly appreciate him, just as I am prepared to be humanly and personally on the best of terms with many another opponent. Emil Brunner is a man whose extraordinary abilities and whose determined will-power I have always sincerely respected. I should like nothing better than to walk together with him in concord, but in the Church we are concerned with truth, and to-day with an urgency such as probably has not been the case for centuries. And truth is not to be trifled with. If it divides the spirits, then they *are* divided. To oppose this commandment for the sake of a general idea of "peace" and "unity" would be a greater disaster for all concerned than such division. Nor must it be a matter for wonder that when this division comes about it appears irrespectively of our formations and groups and appears exceptionally acutely and painfully where before there seemed to be unity, perhaps even far-reaching unity, where perhaps unity really *did* exist or really *can* exist. I can hardly say a clear "No" to Hirsch and his associates, but close my eyes in the case of Brunner, the Calvinist, the Swiss "dialectic theologian." For it seems clear to me that at the decisive point he takes part in the false movement of thought by which the Church to-day is threatened. Is it not true that the danger is greatest where it appears to be least, where error combines with the presentation—a very thorough and skilful presentation—of so many "truths" that at the first, and even at the second and third, glance it looks like the truth itself? My polemic against Brunner is more acute than that against Hirsch because his position is more akin to mine, because I believe him to be in possession of more truth, *i.e.* to be closer to the Scriptures, because I take him more seriously—because for that very reason he seems to me just now to be much more dangerous than a man like Hirsch. The heresies of our time which can be recognised as such at the first glance are, if I am not mistaken, about to go as they have come. Sometimes I am myself amazed that one ever had to defend oneself so explicitly and so decidedly as has been the case in these years. Throughout the struggle which we carried on in these years I have again and again pointed out that the real danger was not to be found in the adversary against whom our struggle was primarily directed. This did not always please the strategists and technicians of the confessional front. The real danger seems to me to lie in a future attitude of the Church and of theology which is informed by the spirit of many on both sides to-day who are undecided and ready for compromise and which might stand at the end of all that we are now going through. Such an end would mean that we would continue comfortably or even busily along the very road which has led us to the present catastrophe and upon which we might meet even greater catastrophes in future. The structure of the Church's proclamation must not remain the sort of thing that it became through the developments of the eighteenth and nineteenth centuries. Especially as regards the problem "Nature and Grace," a breath of fresh air must make an end to the compromises by which we have now lived for so long and from which we had almost died. The Evangelical Church and her theology must emerge from the present suffering and strife purer, more united and more determined than when she entered it. Otherwise she has lost the battle in the midst of which we are standing to-day. Even the blatant abuses which are current to-day will not trouble her any more. The reason why I must resist Brunner so decidedly is that I am thinking of the future theology of compromise, that I regard him as its classical precursor, and that I have heard the applause with which all who are of a like mind have greeted his essay, *Nature and Grace*. His essay is an alarm signal. I wish it had not been written. I wish that this new and greater danger were not approaching or that it had not been Emil Brunner who had crossed my path as an exponent of that danger, in a way which made me feel that for better or for worse I had been challenged. But all this has now happened, and seen in some greater context it probably has its sense. But I hope that since it has happened I shall not be misunderstood if I act according to the use of our times and treat his doctrine of "Nature and Grace" without much ceremony as something which endangers the ultimate truth that must be guarded and defended in the Evangelical Church.

30th October 1934.

I

ANGRY INTRODUCTION

"IT is the task of our theological generation to find the way back to a true *theologia naturalis.*" Thus Emil Brunner in his essay *Nature and Grace: a Contribution to the Discussion with Karl Barth.*

If this is Brunner's opinion—and how can I, how can anyone, doubt any longer that this is indeed the case?— then I fail to understand among many other things the following: how can he think that, in spite of this opinion, he has a right to be mentioned "in one breath" with—of all·people—me, to be my "ally," my "good friend," and that I have merely failed to understand him and therefore have in error shot at him by night? For we ought at least to be at one in defining "the task of our theological generation" if we intended and desired the same thing in the way in which Brunner seems to assume this. How could I deny that I, too, have, as a matter of fact, repeatedly practised "true *theologia naturalis*" in his sense —Brunner has pointed this out—still rather obviously in the essay *Kirche und Kultur* (Church and Culture), 1927, and in some passages of my "Prolegomena" which appeared in the same year? It may be possible to convict me of many atavisms and relapses in this matter, and I am certain that it is not easy to get rid of the demon here in question. But my soul is innocent of ever even having dreamt of the idea that it was a task of our theological generation to find the way back to a "true *theologia naturalis*"! Whether this was the way in which Brunner understood the common origin of our teaching in that of Kutter and Blumhardt, and whether this was his opinion even at the time when I wrote my *Epistle to the*

Romans and he his book about Schleiermacher, or whether this became Brunner's opinion later—in either case both we and our theological contemporaries on both sides of the ocean have been terribly deluded in thinking that we were "loyal comrades in battle." Ever since about 1916, when I began to recover noticeably from the effects of my theological studies and the influences of the liberal-political pre-war theology, my opinion concerning the task of our theological generation has been this: we must learn again to understand revelation as *grace* and grace as *revelation* and therefore turn away from all "true" or "false" *theologia naturalis* by ever making new decisions and being ever controverted anew. When (roughly since 1929) Brunner suddenly began to proclaim openly "the other task of theology," the "point of contact," etc., I made it known that whatever might happen I could and would not agree with this. How could this have been some error occurring at night? If I got rather lively, it was only because I really thought that there was some unity between Brunner and myself and that I could and should warn him against wantonly leaving the strait and narrow path. He may have been astonished at this, but I can tell him now that I then thought that he was still curable. If he knew me—and he must have known me!—he ought not to have been astonished that objectively I could but contradict him. Least of all ought he to try, now that he has made it plain to every eye who he is and what he wants, to continue the "discussion" in the form of an *amica exegesis* and to pretend to the unsuspecting reader that it is really only my genial "one-sidedness," my lack of knowledge of Calvin and my idea that, like William Tell, I am strongest alone, which stands in the way of mutual understanding, *i.e.* of my adhering to Brunner's doctrine. In his essay Brunner has proved that all that he seemed to have learnt fifteen years ago together with me has merely enabled him to return with all the more impetus to that theology of compromise which has shown itself as the cause of the present unhappy state of the Evangelical Church in Germany and which, if things continue in this way, will also bring the other Evangelical Churches to a similar path. The loud applause of K. Fezer, O. Weber, P. Althaus and all the other half- or three-quarter "German Christians" was the thanks he earned for this. The *Deutsche Pfarrerblatt* (*German Pastors' Journal*) (1934, No. 30, p. 377) has called this pamphlet "a mine of treasure, a veritable gold-mine" ("eine Fund—ja geradezu eine Goldgrube"). I am "angry" with Brunner because on top of all this he did not refrain from showering me with love and praise and from maintaining that the matters in which I differ from him are mere "false conclusions." Now I have to reply with a "No!" to Brunner and the whole chorus of his friends and disciples and those who share his opinions. And what a wicked man I appear to be, lacking all communal spirit and stubbornly refusing to allow even the least correction! Brunner might have known how necessary this "No" was and how thorough it had to be. If he considered a "debate" between himself and myself necessary and promising, he might have lent it dignity and status by addressing me from that distance which does as a matter of fact exist between us—however great "a pity" one may consider this. It has happened before that another man at Zurich provoked someone out there in Germany terribly by almost the same methods that Brunner is using now, and he managed to make that man appear for centuries as an intolerant disrupter of Christian unity. I do not wish to compare myself with that man, but when my thoughts go to Zurich I find that I can understand his anger remarkably well. Brunner does not understand or will not understand, or does not wish to show and to say that he understands, that the issue between himself and myself is such that to-day it can only be decided openly and consciously. Since he has thus joined the crowd and has therefore actually become so far removed from me, he might in the name of his Christian profession do me the favour of leaving me in my "isolation" and refrain from informing the world about me in the attitude and tone of a "good friend." It is this obscuring of the situation which makes it so difficult for me to reply to Brunner, that I should like it best to save both my readers and myself the trouble of replying at all. I certainly do not like the rôle of the wicked man which now, for better or for worse, I have to assume. But this unnecessarily complicated aspect of the situation seems to have confused quite a large number of people. It has been impressed upon me from various quarters that I must not keep silent. Someone wrote in the *Bund* of Berne (3rd June 1934) that until Barth replies, "the question of this important discussion flies about like Noah's dove, not knowing where to settle." I do not know whether I shall be able to do anything towards pacifying this dove. But evidently I cannot escape the obligation of doing my utmost. But it should not be held against me if in these pages I appear in a thoroughly exclusive and unfriendly attitude; if the reader now sees an unedifying disruption where before he thought to see unity; and if my answer lacks that "elegance" for which Brunner's essay is praised. At the moment I am not worried about elegance. I have quite different worries. I must become clear and explicit.

II

WHERE DO WE REALLY STAND?

BRUNNER'S "counter-theses," in which he develops his view of a "true" natural theology positively, refer to a series of "theses" in which he attempted with great succinctness and lucidity to explain to himself and to his readers my view of the matter as he understands it and as he wishes to correct it: the image of God in man is totally destroyed by sin. Every attempt to assert a general revelation has to be rejected. There is no grace of creation and preservation. There are no recognisable ordinances of preservation. There is no point of contact for the redeeming action of God. The new creation is in no sense the perfection of the old but rather the replacement of the old man by the new.

That is where I am supposed to stand and to receive Brunner's exhortation and instruction. If I attempt to do this I come immediately upon a fundamental difficulty (quite apart from all the details in which I fail to recognise myself). Not only have I, as Brunner says, never "expounded and defended these theses . . . systematically," but I have never put them forward and do not propose to do so in the future.

By ascribing these theses to me, Brunner imputes to me, apart from all discussion of the pros and cons, a fundamental attitude and position with regard to the whole problem which may be his but is not mine. For I can see no sense in giving to the denial of "natural theology" such systematic attention as appears in these theses. By "natural theology" I mean every (positive *or* negative) *formulation of a system* which claims to be theological, *i.e.* to interpret divine revelation, whose *subject,* however, differs fundamentally from the revelation in Jesus Christ and whose *method* therefore differs equally from the exposition of Holy Scripture. Such a system is contained not only in Brunner's counter-theses but also in the theses ascribed by him to me. Their wording may here and there recall my thoughts and my writings. But this does not mean that I am prepared to accept paternity and responsibility. For they represent—even though negatively—an abstract speculation concerning a something that is not identical with the revelation of God in Jesus Christ. Brunner failed to see that he made a fatal mistake in his initial definitions of my position by treating me as one of his kind. This has made debate difficult, for my first step has to consist in emphasising the distance between us. Or did he want to set me a trap by inviting me to expose myself that way to his counter-theses and thus to make my position as fundamentally questionable as his? However that may be, I do not think of exposing myself like that. For "natural theology" does not exist as an entity capable of becoming a separate subject within what I consider to be real theology—not even for the sake of being rejected. If one occupies oneself with real theology one can pass by so-called natural theology only as one would pass by an abyss into which it is inadvisable to step if one does not want to fall. All one can do is to turn one's back upon it as upon the great temptation and source of error, by having nothing to do with it and by making it clear to oneself and to others from time to time why one acts that way. A real rejection of natural theology does not differ from its acceptance merely in the way in which No differs from Yes. Rather are Yes and No said, as it were, on different levels. Really to reject natural theology means to refuse to admit it as a separate problem. Hence the rejection of natural theology can only be a side issue, arising when serious questions of real theology are being discussed. Real rejection of natural theology does not form part of the creed. Nor does it wish to be an exposition of the creed and of revelation. It is merely an hermeneutical rule, forced upon the exegete by the creed (*e.g.* by the clause *natus ex virgine*) and by revelation. It is not possible to expand and compound it into a system of special tenets explicating and defending it. Rather does it appear necessarily, but with the same dependence as that of shade upon light, at the edge of theology as its necessary limit. If you really reject natural theology you do not stare at the serpent, with the result that it stares back at you, hypnotises you, and is ultimately certain to bite you, but you hit it and kill it as soon as you see it! In all these matters rejection of natural theology differs from its acceptance even before the rejection takes place. Real rejection of natural theology can come about only in the fear of God and hence only be a complete *lack* of interest in this matter. If *this* matter is allowed to become of interest, though but in order to be rejected, then interest is no longer centred upon *theology*. For this rejection cannot within theology be made for its own sake. For it is not by this rejection that truth is known, the Gospel is expounded, God is praised and the Church is built. If all this is to happen at all, then purely and solely by what must take place within the limits set by this rejection. If I were in a position to put forward a series of theses like those attributed to me by Brunner, I should prove thereby that my rejection is not a real rejection at all. Fundamentally I should then have joined Brunner in asserting an "other" task of theology. I should then no longer hold steadfastly to my position. The *drawing* of the limit would then be important to me as such. And if that were the case then I might just as well join Brunner in *transgressing* the limit. I could imagine the contrary also, namely that Brunner might be concerned, not with transgressing the limit but with drawing it, and that he might therefore join me in rejecting natural theology. But I fear—in face of the theses ascribed to me I must really fear—that even then we would from the very start stand in different places and would mean and intend quite different things. In those statements Brunner makes me much too straightforward and doctrinaire, too confident and lacking in reserve. Hence I cannot imagine that Brunner—even a Brunner who might join me in rejecting natural theology—could see how terrible and yet how ineffective this enemy is. Nor could he decide to concentrate upon the one task of true theology which is of paramount concern to me. I fear that, even as an adversary of natural theology, he would always be addicted to an "other" task of theology in addition to that one task and hence he could not be taken seriously as an adversary of natural theology. For of what use would be the purest theology based on grace and revelation to me if I dealt with the subjects of grace and revelation in the way in which natural theology usually deals with its *soi-disant* data derived from reason, nature and history, *i.e.* as if one had them pocketed, as if one had the knowledge of them below one instead of always behind and in front? Could knowledge of them be in that case true, strict, necessary knowledge? Couldn't one in that case afford oneself a little undisguised natural theology? Brunner's explanation of my position would, in my opinion, make me suspicious of him, even if he shared my views. On top of that he thought that he might afford himself a little undisguised natural theology. He maintains and defends it against me. But those who want to be clear as to where he and I really stand and what the issue between us really is, should not rest content with noticing this secondary difference. Our positions differed even before he came to his Yes and I to my No in this matter.

III

BRUNNER'S NATURAL THEOLOGY

In order to form a judgment concerning the positive exposition which Brunner gives to his essay of what he means by natural theology, it is indispensable to consider that under the title of "The issue between Karl Barth and myself":

"We are concerned with the message of the sovereign, freely electing grace of God. Of his free mercy God gives to man, who of himself can do nothing towards his own salvation, to man, whose will is not free but in bondage, his salvation in the Cross of Christ and by the Holy Spirit who enables him to assimilate this word of the Cross. We are therefore also concerned with the freedom of the Church, which has its basis and its justification, its law and its possibility purely and solely in this divine revelation. Therefore it is not tied at all to nations and states. It is above all nations and states without any possibility of accepting from them any law or commission. We are concerned with the fact that the proclamation of the Church has not two sources and norms, such as, *e.g.*, revelation *and* reason or the Word of God *and* history. . . ."

Well, let us proceed. The issue now is this: can the natural theology put forward in Brunner's counter-theses be maintained if measured by the yardstick of his own words? Can these words be taken seriously if viewed against the background of that natural theology?

In order to orientate ourselves provisionally we set over against these words the quintessence of what Brunner wants to teach as "natural theology": there is such a thing as a "capacity for revelation" or "capacity for words" or "receptivity for words" or "possibility of being addressed" which man possesses even apart from

revelation.   It would   seem   that   even   the   first   naïve
impression   would   be   that   either   the   first   or   the   second
pronouncement has to be strangely watered down if they
are to be able to stand side by side.   What is the meaning
of "sovereign, freely electing grace of God " if without it
there is a "capacity for revelation" in man, which is
merely supported by grace?   What is the meaning of
"receptivity for words" if man can do nothing of himself
for his salvation, if it is the Holy Spirit that gives him
living knowledge of the word of the Cross?   But let us
turn to Brunner's own thoughts:

(1) Man's capacity for revelation means, according to
Brunner, his "likeness to God."   "Man's undestroyed
formal likeness to God is the objective possibility of the
revelation of God."   Brunner points out that what matters
is   the   purely   formal   factor   distinctive   of   man   within
creation, the "humanum," the fact that man is a subject,
his   rationality,   his   responsibility,   which   is   the   presupposition of his ability to believe as well as to sin.
This presupposition, the "quod of personality," is not
abolished by sin.   In this formal sense the original image
of God in man is not destroyed.   Indeed not, we may well
say.   Even as a sinner man is man and not a tortoise.
But does this mean that his reason is therefore more
"suited" for defining the nature of God than anything
else in the world?   What is the relevance of the "capacity
for revelation" to the fact that man is man?   The
impression given by Brunner's essay has been described
roughly like this.   If a man had just been saved from
drowning by a competent swimmer, would it not be
very unsuitable if he proclaimed the fact that he was a
man and not a lump of lead as his "capacity for being
saved"?   Unless he could claim to have helped the man
who saved him by a few strokes or the like!   Can Brunner
mean that?   Surely not, for we heard of "man of himself
can do nothing for his salvation."   And according to

Brunner, "the possibility of doing . . . that which is good
in the sight of God" is also lost. One would have thought
that this included the possibility of receiving the revelation
of God. "Materially the *imago* is completely lost, man
is a sinner through and through, and there is nothing in
him which is not defiled by sin." In face of these strong
words it would seem that we have no right to ascribe to
Brunner the view that the "capacity for revelation"
means that man, as it were, works in concert with the
grace which comes to him in revelation. But if he does
not mean that, what *does* he mean by "capacity for
revelation"? It is obvious that man is a responsible
person, even as a sinner. If it is honestly not proposed to
go beyond stating this formal fact, how can the assertion
of this fact serve at all to make revelation something more
than divine grace? Is Brunner able to say one word
beyond what is so obvious, without involving himself in
contradiction with his unconditional acceptance of the
Reformers' principle of *sola scriptura—sola gratia*?

(2) Brunner next asserts that the world is "somehow
recognisable" to man as the creation of God, that "men
somehow know the will of God." "The creation of the
world is at the same time revelation, self-communication
of God." And the possibility of recognising it as such is
adversely affected but not destroyed by sin. It is not
enough to give such knowledge of God as will bring
salvation. Moreover, the revelation of God in nature can
be known "in all its magnitude" only by him "whose
eyes have been opened by Christ." But it is "somehow"
recognisable—though but distortedly and dimly—even
by those of whom this cannot be said. The idea that
revelation is "recognisable" dominates the beginning of
that section. But Brunner also says that surprisingly
enough "sin makes man *blind* for what is visibly set before
our eyes." This makes it not quite clear whether Brunner
does not wish to speak of a purely formal possibility of

knowing God through his creation, which is not actualised. But I think that I understand Brunner rightly when I assume that the affection of the eyes, of which he speaks, is, according to his opinion, very acute, but not to the extent of resulting in total blindness. Hence real knowledge of God through creation does take place without revelation, though only "somehow" and "not in all its magnitude." I think this interpretation is correct. If it is not, I cannot think what Brunner's exposition of the matter intends to convey. Therefore in view of what was said above about the total loss of the "material" *imago*, one is tempted to think that when in this context Brunner speaks of "God" and his "revelation" he means one of those creatures of man's philosophical phantasy, one of those principalities and powers of the world of ideas and demons, which most certainly do exist and which reveal themselves and are known to us quite concretely. For if man "can do nothing of himself for his salvation," they alone can be the objects of his *de facto* knowledge of God through nature! But what Brunner says and means is different. What would be the significance of the assertion of *such* a knowledge of "God" for his thesis concerning man's capacity for revelation? It would mean that the God revealed in nature is *not* known to, but rather is very much hidden from, man. What would then become of the *theologia naturalis*? All that would be left would be a systematic exposition of the history of religion, philosophy and culture, without any theological claims or value. No, when he speaks of the God who can be and is "somehow" known through creation, Brunner does unfortunately mean the one true God, the triune creator of heaven and earth, who justifies us through Christ and sanctifies us through the Holy Spirit. It is he who is *de facto* known by all men without Christ, without the Holy Spirit, though knowledge of him is

F

distorted and dimmed and darkened by sin, though he is "misrepresented" and "turned into idols." There are two kinds of revelation, both revealing the one true God. This is to be affirmed once and for all (on the basis of Scripture!). Only after that may it be asked "how the two revelations, that in creation and that in Jesus Christ, are related." But if that is Brunner's opinion, shall we be able to understand him otherwise than "somehow" distortedly, dimly and darkly? Is it his opinion that idolatry is but a somewhat imperfect preparatory stage of the service of the true God? Is the function of the revelation of God merely that of leading us from one step to the next within the all-embracing reality of divine revelation? Moreover, how can Brunner maintain that a real knowledge of the true God, however imperfect it may be (and what knowledge of God is not imperfect?) does not bring salvation? And if we really do know the true God from his creation without Christ and without the Holy Spirit—if this is so, how can it be said that the *imago* is materially "entirely lost," that in matters of the proclamation of the Church Scripture is the only norm, and that man can do nothing towards his salvation? Shall we not have to ascribe to him the ability to prepare himself for the knowledge of God in Christ at least negatively? Shall we not have to do what Roman Catholic theology has always done and ascribe to him a *potentia oboedientialis* which he possesses from creation and retains in spite of sin? Has not Brunner added to man's "capacity for revelation," to what we have been assured is purely "formal," something very material: man's practically proved ability to know God, imperfectly it may be, but nevertheless really and therefore surely not without relevance to salvation? Perhaps he can swim a little, after all? If he has really done this, we are happy to know now more clearly what he means by "capacity for revelation." But how can Brunner wish to do this? The echo of his audible confession of the Reformers' doctrines of original sin, justification and the Scriptures is still sounding in our ears! Then he does *not* want to do it? But if not, then what *does* he want to do? No, after all, we still remain rather unhappy.

(3) Next, Brunner asserts a special "preserving grace," *i.e.* the preserving and helping presence which God does not deny even to the fallen and estranged creature. We could easily understand this if Brunner meant to say that it is due to grace that after the fall man and his world exist at all or do not exist in a much worse state of disruption than is actually the case. Creation is the work of the truly free, truly undeserved grace of the one true God, both as an act *and* in its continuance. All very well, we can say. But by what right and in what sense does Brunner speak of another special (or rather "general") grace which as it were precedes the grace of Jesus Christ? If this were not so (but as Brunner wishes to obtain a separate *theologia naturalis* it *has* to be so), one could come to an understanding with Brunner. We could agree that the grace of Jesus Christ includes the patience with which God again and again gives us time for repentance and for the practice of perseverance, the patience by which he upholds and preserves man and his world, not for his own sake but for the sake of Christ, for the sake of the Church, for the sake of the elect children of God. We have time, because Christ ever intercedes for us before the judgment-seat of God. How can the preservation of man's existence and of the room given him for it be understood as the work of the one true God unless one means thereby that man is preserved through Christ for Christ, for repentance, for faith, for obedience, for the preservation of the Church? How can it be understood unless baptism is taken into account? How can one speak of these things unless the one revelation of Christ in the Old and New Testaments

is taken into account? And how can one carry the severance of creation and reconciliation into the Bible? Does not the Bible relate all that Brunner calls a special "preserving grace" to prophecy and fulfilment, to law and gospel, to the covenant and the Messiah, to Israel and to the Church, to the children of God and their future redemption? Where did Brunner read of another abstract preserving grace? But since he insists on it we must go on to ask how far his "preserving grace" is grace at all. We are ever and again allowed to exist under various conditions which at least moderate the worst abuses. Does that deserve to be called "grace"? Taken by itself it might just as well be our condemnation to a kind of antechamber of hell! If it is anything else— as indeed it is—then not on account of our preservation as such! We must go on to ask: Can we really know that our preservation as such, *e.g.* "what we derive from our people and their history," is a special grace of the one true God? Does this not mean that the principle *sola scriptura* which Brunner accepts, most inopportunely blocks an important source of knowledge? Does it not mean that the Church cannot possibly have her basis and her justification, her law and her possibility, purely and solely in divine revelation? Does it not mean—am I dreaming?—that the poor "German Christians" may have been treated most unfairly? We must go on to ask: are not both the preservation of our existence as such and its conditions—Brunner mentions, *e.g.*, the State— so much bound up with our own human possibilities that it cannot be said of this "grace" that man can of himself do nothing towards it? Brunner himself declares: "Consequently human activity comes within the purview of divine grace—not of redeeming but of preserving grace. All activity of man, which the creator himself uses to preserve his creation amid the corruptions of sin, belongs to this type of activity within preserving grace."

Human activity which the creator uses to carry out the
work of his grace? This concept is intelligible on the
basis of the Augustinian idea of the indirect identity of
human and divine activity or of the Thomist idea of the
co-operation of the divine *causa materialis* with a human
causa instrumentalis. It might be favourably understood
if Brunner were speaking of the one justifying and
sanctifying grace of Jesus Christ. For in that case also
human activity "comes within the purview of divine
grace." But that is not what Brunner wants. He wishes
to speak of a special "preserving grace"! Has he not by
so doing included in his doctrine an entire sphere (one
which is, as it were, preparatory to revelation in the
proper sense) in which the Reformers' principle of *sola
gratia* cannot possibly be taken seriously? If there really
is such a sphere of preparation, will this leave the understanding of revelation proper unaffected? Once Brunner
has started to deal in abstractions such as these, will he
be able to refrain from joining the Romanists, enthusiasts
and pietists of all times in teaching also a special grace of
life, a special grace of realisation, etc., for which God
"uses" man no less than in the sphere of preparation?
And *where* is all this going to lead us?

(4) Brunner's fourth assertion is partly an exposition
of the third. It treats separately of the "ordinances,"
the "constant factors of historical and social life . . .
without which no communal life is conceivable, which
could in any way be termed human." But among them
he wishes to ascribe to matrimony as an "ordinance of
creation" a "higher dignity" than to the State which is a
mere "ordinance of preservation" relative to sin. Of the
"ordinances of creation" it is said that "through the
preserving grace of God they are *known* also to natural
man as ordinances that are necessary and somehow holy
and are by him *respected* as such." Of matrimony in
particular it is said that "it is realised to some extent by

men who are ignorant of the God revealed in Christ."
The believer understands these ordinances of creation
"better" than the unbeliever; he even understands them
"rightly" and "perfectly." Nevertheless even the believer
"cannot but allow his instinct and his reason to function
with regard to these ordinances, just as in the arts." What
can one say to that? No doubt there are such things
as moral and sociological axioms which seem to underlie
the various customs, laws and usages of different peoples,
and seem to appear in them with some regularity. And
there certainly seems to be some connection between
these axioms and the instinct and reason which both
believers and unbelievers have indeed every reason to
allow to function in the life of the community. But what
are these axioms? Or who—among us, who are "sinners
through and through"!—decides what they are? If we
consulted instinct and reason, what might or might not
be called matrimony? Do instinct and reason really tell
us what is *the* form of matrimony, which would then have
to be acknowledged and proclaimed as a divine ordinance
of creation? If we were chiefly concerned with the clarity
and certainty of knowledge, would not the physical,
biological and chemical "laws of nature" or certain
axioms of mathematics have a much greater claim to
being called ordinances of creation than those historico-
social constants? And who or what raises these constants
to the level of commandments, of binding and authoritative demands, which, as divine ordinances, they would
obviously have to be? Instinct and reason? And what
yardstick have we for measuring these sociological
"ordinances of creation," arranging them in a little
hierarchy and ascribing to one a greater, to the other a
lesser, "dignity"? Do we as "believers" sit in the
councils of God? Are we able to decide such a question?
On the basis of instinct and reason one man may proclaim one thing to be an "ordinance of creation," another

another thing—according to the liberal, conservative or revolutionary inclinations of each. Can such a claim be anything other than the rebellious establishment of some very private *Weltanschauung* as a kind of papacy? Do theologians do well in taking part in one of these rebellions and in giving their blessing to them by proclaiming them to be divinely necessary? But let us assume for the moment that Brunner is right and that we possess some criterion for establishing here and there divine "ordinances of creation" on the basis of instinct and reason. What are we then to think of Brunner's assertion that these ordinances of creation are not only known but also respected and "to some extent realised" by men who do not know the God revealed in Christ? Of what Christian, however faithful, can it be said that he "to some extent realised" the ordinances of God? Is he not "a sinner through and through"—who would be lost if the law were not realised—but not merely "to some extent" but completely, finally and sufficiently for us all!—in Christ? If man can realise the law "to some extent" without Christ, how much more must "capacity for revelation" mean than merely the formal fact of man being human, *i.e.* a responsible and rational subject! Where, where has the distinction of the formal and the material *imago* got to? It is now purely arbitrary to continue to say that only holy Scripture may be the standard of the Church's message, that man can do nothing for his salvation, that it takes place *sola gratia*, that the Church must be free from all national and political restrictions! If man is from the start, and without the revelation and grace of Christ even "to some extent" on such good terms with God, if he can swim enough to help his deliverer by making a few good strokes—if all this is so, why are we suddenly so exclusive?

(5) The pot is boiling over. Brunner's aims in the whole matter are beginning to show up: there is a "point

of contact" for redeeming grace. What is meant is evidently the "capacity for revelation," which is anterior to, though it only comes alive through, revelation. Brunner proceeds to discuss this "capacity for revelation" from the point of view that it is the basis on which the Word of God "reaches" man. Thus Brunner returns to his original definition: the point of contact is "the formal *imago Dei* which not even the sinner has lost, the fact that man is man, the *humanitas*." In order to be responsible and capable of making a decision—as is presupposed by revelation—man must have "the formal possibility of being addressed." We have already pointed out how unsuitable this definition is for what Brunner wishes to prove. If we are prepared to call the fact that man is man and not a cat the "point of contact," "the objective possibility of divine revelation," then all objection to these concepts is nonsensical. For this truth is incontrovertible. Even so, it would be advisable to be careful about statements such as that man alone is capable of receiving the Word of God, because this leaves the angels out of account, because there might, after all, exist beings that are unknown to us, and because we have no revelation but only conjectures concerning receptivity or lack of receptivity on the part of such non-human beings as we do know. But be that as it may: what is the relevance of the formal responsibility and ability to make decisions to a "capacity" which man possesses and which exists in him anterior to divine revelation? Is the revelation of God some kind of "matter" to which man stands in some original relation because as man he *has* or even *is* the "form" which enables him to take responsibility and make decisions in relation to various kinds of "matter"? Surely all his rationality, responsibility and ability to make decisions might yet go hand in hand with complete impotency as regards *this* "matter"! And this impotency might be the tribulation and affliction of those who, as far as human reason can see, possess neither reason, responsibility nor ability to make decisions: new-born children and idiots. Are they not children of Adam? Has Christ not died for them? The fact that God "reaches" man with his Word may well be due to something other than the formal possibility of his being addressed and his *humanitas*. If we are going to stick to the statement that man is ("materially") "a sinner through and through," then the "formal factor" cannot be anything like a remainder of some original righteousness, an openness and readiness for God. The concept of a "capacity" of man for God has therefore to be dropped. If, nevertheless, there is an encounter and communion between God and man, then God himself must have created for it conditions which are not in the least supplied (not even "somehow," not even "to some extent"!) by the existence of the formal factor. But we have seen that Brunner unfortunately has no intention of stopping at this formal factor. The reason for this is that he departs from the statement that man is "a sinner through and through," thus contradicting the exposition which precedes it. For he has by now also "materially" enriched and adorned man in his relation to God to an amazing extent. "The sphere of this possibility of being addressed" includes not only the *humanum* in the narrower sense, but everything connected with the "natural" knowledge of God. Moreover, "the necessary, indispensable point of contact," which before was defined as the "*formal imago Dei*," has now, as it were, openly become "what the natural man knows of God, of the law, and of his own dependence upon God." From afar there sounds across to us like the last echoes of thunder when a storm has passed by without doing harm: "This quid of personality is negatived through sin." No doubt the distinction between the "formal" and the "material" *imago Dei*, which at first sight was so impressive, was not meant all that seriously, even in those early passages. The form was probably quite a well-filled form even there. Evidently the "formal *imago Dei*" meant that man can "somehow" and "to some extent" know and do the will of God without revelation. If we had been acute enough to know that right from the start, we should have saved ourselves our amazement at the irrelevance of the statement that man is man! How very relevant and full of import it was! But we are not really guilty, since Brunner gave us no indications in this direction and, moreover, had explicitly assured us that he would adhere to the principle *sola scriptura—sola gratia*. That has not happened. If it had happened, it would not have been possible to set man over against God, either secretly or openly, as a form that is "somehow" already filled. In that case the purely formal statement that man is man would have been seen to be irrelevant and— would not have been made at all or at least not so solemnly! The question of the "point of contact" might then have occurred to Brunner in the context of the doctrine of Christ, of the Spirit, of the Church, but not of man. Brunner has been unable to adhere to *sola fide—sola gratia*. He has entered upon the downward path, upon which we find him in *Nature and Grace* more obviously than in any previous pronouncement. Why then is he angry with me because my objection— which indeed has a wide scope—is that I am no longer able to distinguish him fundamentally from a Thomist or Neo-Protestant? In addition to the applause of the "German Christians" and their ilk he should make a point of reading what my Roman Catholic colleague at Bonn, Gottlieb Söhngen, wrote concerning his under-taking (*Catholica*, 1934, No. 3, p. 113 ff.). This should convince him that I am not wantonly branding him as a heretic, but that this really is how the matter stands.

(6) For a moment Brunner seems to have occupied

himself after all with the possibility—upon which we
have already touched—that the answer to his question
might be found in the doctrine of Christ, of the Holy
Spirit, of the Church. For he turns to the theme of the
death of the old Adam as a condition of the life of the
new Adam, to whom the revelation of God is made.
Now he remembers Galatians ii, 20: "I live; yet not I,
but Christ liveth in me," and 1 Corinthians ii, 10 f.:
"But God hath revealed them unto us by his Spirit."
But it is now that we meet with the worst surprise. In
the counter-theses 2-5 Brunner's view of man's capacity
for revelation has become perfectly clear. Moreover,
even without revelation man somehow knows God and,
to some extent, fulfils his will. Might we not now expect
to be shown how this view is justified and proved when
confronted with these two texts? Instead of that, Brunner
returns to his original definition of "capacity for
revelation" which he had since abandoned. It now
signifies the undoubted and indubitable formal definition
of man as a self-conscious person. And he uses these
passages quite superfluously to prove that the death of the
old Adam refers always to the material but never to the
formal aspect of human nature. The subject as such and
the fact of its self-consciousness are not abolished by
faith. Faith is not mysticism. The believer does not
become Christ. Through the Holy Spirit an act of
divine self-consciousness takes place within us, without,
however, resulting in an identity between him and us.
We receive the Holy Spirit, but our personal identity
remains. Who would not agree with that? Though in
contrast to an excessively Swiss sobriety some might wish
to put in a good word for mysticism and maintain that
the act of faith sometimes has taken place and may well
take place in mystical forms of consciousness. But apart
from that, Brunner would have to be opposed on the
following grounds: what he has to prove is that in these

passages the life of man in Christ through the Holy
Spirit is said to *presuppose* a knowledge of and respect for
the true God and that this presupposition forms its *point
of contact* in man. Where in Galatians ii and 1 Corinthians
ii has Brunner found anything of the sort? Which of the
sixteen verses of 1 Corinthians ii could be quoted to
show that St. Paul wanted to maintain and proclaim
another knowledge of God before and beside "Jesus
Christ and him crucified" (v. 2), before and beside the
"demonstration of the Spirit and of power" (v. 4),
before and beside "the hidden wisdom in a mystery"
(v. 7), before and beside the "revelation by the Spirit"
(v. 10)—and not merely as another knowledge beside
all these, but as their presupposition and point of contact? In 1 Corinthians ii, St. Paul seems clearly to
assume that something of the sort exists. But he does
not do so in the way in which Brunner does. Rather does
he regard it as "the wisdom of men" (vv. 5 and 13), as
"the spirit of the world" (v. 12), as the ability of
"psychical (natural) man" who does not accept "the
things of the Spirit of God," who instead regards them
as "foolishness" because "he *cannot* know them" (v. 14).
Of what use is man's "formal personality"—which St.
Paul does not deny—to him? What did St. Paul find in
him that might have been of interest to him as a capacity
for revelation or a point of contact? In Galatians ii,
15-21, St. Paul declares that he is crucified with Christ
and dead to the law and that he therefore lives but now
only in the faith of the Son of God given for him. He does
not deny the continuance of his "formal personality."
But is it of any importance to him? Does not the context
show clearly that, in spite of this continuance, St. Paul
speaks in verse 20 not of continuity but of discontinuity,
or rather of the divine miracle of the continuity of his
existence without and with Christ, apart from and in
Christ? Moreover the text does not go on to say something

that it would have to say if Brunner could fittingly quote
it in his support. It does not say that though St. Paul is
crucified with Christ, but that nevertheless, together with
his "formal personality," some general knowledge of
God derived from his conscience or from the ordinances
of creation, recognisable in the world, accompanied or
even led him into that new life which he can but try to
explain by the inexplicable expression: "Christ liveth
in me." Does he live the life which he lives "in the flesh,"
the first life, crucified with Christ, in any way but "in the
faith of the Son of God, who loved me and gave himself
for me"? Is the change in the human situation through
the revelation of God, of which 1 Corinthians ii and
Galatians ii speak, really a *reparatio*, a restoration in
the sense in which Brunner employs it: "It is not possible
to repair what no longer exists. *But it is possible to repair
a thing in such a way that one has to say this has become quite
new*"? (Italics mine.) I must confess that I am quite
flabbergasted by this sentence. Had one not better at
this point break off the discussion as hopeless? Or should
one hope for an angel from heaven who would call to
Brunner through a silver trumpet of enormous dimensions
that 2 Corinthians v, 17, is not a mere phrase, which
might just as well be applied to a motor-car that has come
to grief and been successfully "repaired"? Or should
one implore Brunner to turn his attention again to his
rejection of the doctrine of the virgin birth, in order to
see from this doctrine—which has been so much misunderstood both by him and by others—what that
"hidden wisdom in a mystery" (1 Cor. ii, 7) is about,
which one has to know if one wants to be able to discuss
nature and grace? Or should one ask him to read again
quietly the texts which he himself quotes, 1 Corinthians ii
and Galatians ii (and surely also 2 Cor. v) in order to
convince himself that *that reparatio*, which is mentioned
there, is one in which there can be no question of a

capacity for repair on the part of man. This is because the "repair" consists in a *miracle* performed upon man, in a miracle which makes it not a phrase but literal truth to say that he has become a new man, a new creature— because his "formal" aptitude for it is the most *uninteresting* and his "material" aptitude the most *impossible* thing in the world and hence they cannot be problems.

I break off. In Brunner's theology there is as little room for both evangelical and natural theology as anywhere where an attempt has been made to combine those two. And similarly, as always, so in the case of Brunner the conflict ended unequivocally in favour of natural theology. There is no doubt that Brunner could and can go further on the road that he has taken, than he has done so far. I do not know what he proposes to do next. It seems that behind his re-introduction of natural theology a "new" doctrine of the Holy Spirit wants only too logically to break forth. Against this doctrine it will be even more necessary to protest. I do not know whether my words have the power of warning him and making him stop. What is certain is that on *this* road things can only become worse and worse, *i.e.* he cannot but move further and further away from the postulates of evangelical thought which he himself has set down at the beginning of his essay.

IV

BRUNNER AND CALVIN

BRUNNER is of the opinion that his natural theology "adheres to the teaching of the Reformation" and is "quite near Calvin's doctrine," and that conversely Calvin's doctrine is at least usually "more or less" the same as his own doctrine of the formal side of the *imago Dei*.

The place where I am writing this chapter is not a little apt to stimulate the imagination with regard to the perspectives which would open up to us if Brunner were right. For I am sitting at an open window on the Monte Pincio in Rome. Over there I can see St. Peter's quite clearly. Could I not, must I not—always assuming that Brunner's doctrine "adheres to the teaching of the Reformation"—ask, if not the *analogia entis* personally then at least one of the *savants* of over there, for an interview and draw his attention to the fact that the relation of Roman Catholic and Evangelical theology has for all too long a time been burdened by a serious mutual misunderstanding and that the time seems to have come for clearing that misunderstanding away?

I would, however, have to betray Brunner in one respect. For I would have to concede that his representation of the Roman Catholic conception of the nature and significance of natural theology is sadly distorted. No one who has even to a small extent studied St. Thomas or the formulations of the Vatican Decree, or who has discussed these matters with a Roman Catholic theologian of any erudition, will be able to say that according to Roman Catholic doctrine there is an "unrefracted *theologia naturalis*" with which sin "has as it were nothing to do," a system of natural theology, a self-sufficient rational system, detachable from the *theologia revelata* and capable of serving it for a solid foundation. How can Brunner make this out to be Roman Catholic doctrine: "The *theologia naturalis* is derivable from reason alone," by which nature, *i.e.* the divine order of creation, is entirely and adequately comprehensible and accessible? Every Roman Catholic theologian who knows his subject at all must and will reject Brunner's description of his position as a basis for discussion. He need not even be one of those who have the Protestant objection before their eyes as clearly as is now at least sometimes the case in Germany, France and Belgium. He will reject it because, according to Roman Catholic theology, conditioned as it is by St. Thomas (and which therefore incorporates almost all of Augustine!), a true knowledge of God derived from reason and nature is *de facto* never attained without prevenient and preparatory grace. There can be no question of separating nature and grace "neatly . . . by a horizontal line." Rather does nature presuppose grace, supernatural revelation as the sphere of relevant theological knowledge and statements, in the same way in which grace presupposes nature. According to the Roman Catholic, reason, if left entirely without grace, is incurably sick and incapable of any serious theological activity. Only when it has been illumined, or at least provisionally shone upon by faith, does reason serve to produce those statements concerning God, man and the world, which, according to Roman Catholic doctrine, are not only articles of revelation but have to be considered as truths of reason. Neither the doctrine of grace which has come from the Augustinian-Thomist school, nor the Roman Catholic doctrine of knowledge which has been brought into accord with it, is as crudely Pelagian as some Protestant controverialists would make it out to be, both for the sake of simplicity and—for the sake of covering their own weaknesses. Many imprudent people on our side would do well to see to it that—within the view of the systematic co-ordination of nature and grace, which is common to Roman Catholics and Neo-Protestants—they are not suddenly excelled by the Romans in seriousness and profundity and urgency of this or that thought. They should see to it that the truth of predestination does not suddenly turn out to have been much better preserved by the others than by themselves! This would be what I should have to concede to my *vis-à-vis* in the discussion. Roman Catholic *theologia naturalis* in present-day authoritative Roman Catholic theology is certainly not what Brunner and some others take it to be.

But after that the discussion could proceed very happily and full of promise. Assuming that Brunner's natural theology "adheres to the teaching of the Reformation," I could explain to the man over there that until now he has had quite a false idea of the evangelical and reformed doctrine of *theologia naturalis*. I should say that this false impression was probably due to certain harsh expressions of Luther's, *e.g.* in his exposition of the Epistle to the Romans, due especially to what he had thought he knew about Calvin, due also to certain "one-sided" and pointed assertions on the part of contemporary Protestant theologians. Up to now, I should say to him, you have no doubt thought that, according to evangelical doctrine, there can be as little question of a co-operation of reason in the knowledge of the true God, as of a co-operation of the human will in the fulfilment of the divine commandments—not even with the proviso that the work of prevenient and preparatory grace be taken into account. Until now you honestly believed that, according to evangelical doctrine, human reason is as blind to the truth of God as the human will is unfree to do what is right before God and that, according to our doctrine, light and freedom could be found exclusively in faith, *i.e.* in Jesus Christ. Up to now you have turned away from these hard words with horror and have emphasised against them that man is here lowered in an almost Manichæan fashion and God is in a shocking and dangerous way turned into a distant and incomprehensible God. Now you may, and indeed must, abandon this picture of our position and the corresponding polemic against it. It is indeed true that we stress the point that a "true" *theologia naturalis* can exist only where man's eyes have been opened by Christ.

G

The *lex naturae* has again to be "made perfectly clear" through Scripture. "The ordinances of creation and nature are also somewhat obscured by sin and need to be made known again by Christ." But does not this coincide with what you know and are accustomed to say in this context concerning prevenient grace, concerning the illumination of reason through grace, etc.? We are at one in thinking of man in spite of the fall as being in safe and continued possession of a rational nature and of immortality, an aptitude for culture, a conscience, responsibility and a relation to God, etc. (even though the last does not of itself bring salvation). Hence grace *can* give him real and true knowledge of God and *does* give it him in such a way that apart from the new "supernatural" knowledge, derived from the revelation of God in Christ, those "forms" are filled in such a way "that one has to say: this has become quite new." Therefore we have after all a "true" *theologia naturalis* side by side with *theologia revelata* as "an important complement of the knowledge of God derived from Scripture." Nor shall we miss the opportunity of putting this complement to the widest possible use in our ethics. You are amazed, my good Roman Catholic friend. Perhaps you have a suspicion that these might merely be the views of some Neo-Protestant and therefore not to be considered binding, while the main force of Protestantism, supported by the Reformers themselves, might stand in quite a different place? But abandon your suspicions. Understand that—quite apart from the authority of Brunner—what I have been telling you is in the main nothing but the genuine teaching of the fierce and terrible Calvin, whom you would hardly have suspected of such a thing and from whom "we" had merely failed to enquire soon enough. But now we *have* enquired! Read Brunner's 126 quotations from Calvin and look forward to the as yet unpublished work of his

pupil, G. Gloede, in which you will find an absolutely
"enormous number of references" of the same kind.
See for yourself that this doctrine which appears so
terrifying at the first glance is in reality quite mild and
synthetic and neatly overlooks and systematically co-
ordinates God and man, nature and grace, reason and
revelation. And thus you may convince yourself—if even
Calvin says so, who would doubt?—that this doctrine
"adheres to the teaching of the Reformation" and is the
genuine doctrine of the Evangelical Church. What is
there that still divides us? Certainly we are not as yet
able to express everything as completely, as clearly, as
consequently as your Przywara. When concepts fail us,
we have as yet frequently to have recourse to the word
"somehow." As yet we do not understand each other
fully. But where is there any really fundamental division?
But if in the sphere of the doctrine of knowledge an
understanding between us is not impossible, surely a
similar understanding would necessarily follow in the
sphere of the doctrine of grace. Perhaps all that is
necessary in this matter also is that we should calmly
listen to one another. Might we not notice then that in
this matter too we are not so far apart? What prospects!
What hopes! Of course the "German Christians" have
been very glad about the new discovery of what "adheres
to the teaching of the Reformation." Of course we are
now able and indeed forced to concede more to their position than many "one-sided" people, who have not yet
understood this new discovery, are prepared to allow. But
I am sure that this will not disturb you . . .! That is what
I should have to say, in spirit addressing the Vatican
from the Monte Pincio, if—if only Brunner's appeal to
the Reformers, and especially to Calvin, were in order.

But I am not able to make that speech, for Brunner's
appeal is not in order. Of the many amazing things in
his essay this is to me one of the most amazing, that he

has dared to introduce the figure of Calvin. Was it really necessary that he should burden his thesis and our discussion with this historical assertion, which is as astonishing as it is confusing? Well, it has happened, and the question which has thus arisen will have to be dealt with, whether we like it or not. Since I am not a Calvin scholar in the stricter sense of the word, and since the necessary investigation and exposition would exceed the limit of this essay, I have asked my brother, Peter Barth, to inform the readers of *Theologische Existenz heute* concerning the problem of natural theology in the teaching of Calvin in a separate issue, in the same way in which Ernst Wolf has done it for Luther in No. 6. Even now it is highly profitable to read what Peter Brunner has written in the periodical, *Evangelische Theologie*, 1934, No. 6, p. 189 ff., under the title "Allgemeine und besondere Offenbarung in Calvin's *Institutio*" ("General and particular Revelation in Calvin's *Institutes*"). This was written in view of Emil Brunner's thesis, although not explicitly dealing with it. Provisionally and summarily the reasons for my own rejection of Brunner's appeal to Calvin are the following:

It seems to me above all to rest fundamentally upon an insufficient appreciation of the place of the Reformers in the history of dogma. For with regard to the problem of natural theology that place is characterised by the fact that in their controversy with Roman Catholicism the Reformers were, according to the former's theological constitution at the time (apart from the *Sentences* of Peter Lombard), faced with the very questionable pelagianising formulations of the later Nominalism. They did not know—or knew only superficially—the superior systematic method and harmony with which St. Thomas Aquinas had developed the principle: *Gratia non tollit sed praesupponit et perficit naturam—Santa Maria sopra Minerva*, to let the *genius loci* speak once more! The same historical position may also be expressed thus: The Reformers did not perceive the extent to which even *Augustine*, to whom they were so fond of appealing, has to be regarded as a Roman Catholic theologian, and the reserve with which he has therefore to be taken. Hence they were not in a position to foresee all the reservations with which Roman Catholic theology has since, *i.e.* since the rediscovery of St. Thomas, learnt to surround its (materially unchanged) definitions. For the substance of these definitions has since, in an idealist form, *i.e.* in that of a secularised Thomism (which has found its mature form in Schleiermacher's *Glaubenslehre*—E.T. *The Christian Faith*), but without consciousness of its real connections, become part of the armoury of modernist Protestantism. If we really wish to maintain the Reformers' position over against that of Roman Catholicism and Neo-Protestantism, we are not in a position to-day to repeat the statements of Luther and Calvin without at the same time making them more pointed than they themselves did. This applies also to the doctrine of grace, *e.g.* in the definition of the relation between justification and sanctification. But the practical non-existence of St. Thomas in the sixteenth century has had even graver consequences, in that the Reformers could not clearly perceive the range of the decisive connection which exists in the Roman Catholic system between the problem of justification and the problem of the knowledge of God, between reconciliation and revelation. They remained essentially untouched by the great syntheses of St. Thomas, which later gained such great influence. Hence they did not feel themselves called upon to clarify the problem of the *formal* relation between reason with its interpretation of nature and history on the one hand and the absolute claims of revelation on the other, in the same way in which they treated the material problem of the relation between the will and work of man and the reconciliation once and for all effected in Christ. In their controversy with Roman Catholicism they were content, in matters formal, to indicate their new understanding of the grace of God by means of asserting and working out the scriptural principle over against the principle of tradition. Apart from a few attempts in this direction, they did not characterise as such or emphasise the disagreement between the Evangelical and the Roman Catholic *knowledge* of God which arises out of the former disagreement. They saw and attacked the possibility of an intellectual work-righteousness in the basis of theological thought. But they did not do so as widely, as clearly and as fundamentally as they did with respect to the possibility of a moral work-righteousness in the basis of Christian life. Thus, for example, Calvin's *Institutes* is one of the few works of the Reformers in which the problem of knowledge is raised to any extent. In the famous introduction to this work pagan philosophy is said to reach, even at its best, but a false knowledge of God. But we find no explicit rejection of the temptation to look for a possible core of truth which might yet be found in the pre-Christian knowledge of God and to co-ordinate it systematically with the Christian knowledge of God—by calling it a preparation or the like—with the result that it becomes the framework and secret law of the latter. In order to understand that this would really be impossible for Calvin, one has to consider his doctrine of Christ, of the unfree will, of justification, but above all the fact that in treating of classical pagan philosophy he did not make this systematic inclusion, that, in fact, he spoke only of the theological *in*capacity of "natural" man. It is not possible, however, to find in those introductory chapters any direct and explicit delimitation of Calvin's method against that of Thomism. This is the little piece of truth by which Brunner lives. It seems that Calvin did not know the Thomist method

or that it did not interest him. It is therefore not physic-
ally and mechanically impossible to precipitate oneself
into that little corner which has been left uncovered in
Calvin's treatment, and to supplement his rejection of
Cicero's natural theology by putting forward a dialectical
theology of nature and grace. One may furthermore
make out that this theology "adheres to the teaching of
the Reformation" because it is possible to utilise for its
construction all manner of Calvinistic fragments—sentences and parts of sentences, from which it is evident
that Calvin was, as it were, not thinking of St. Thomas
at all and of Augustine only by way of seriously misunderstanding him. That is what Brunner has done. In
this manner he thinks he can prove it. And that is what
I take so much amiss. One cannot take it amiss that
Abraham Kuyper, a child of the eighteenth and nineteenth centuries, once went a similar way in his exposition
of Calvin—more so than he himself knew. But a few
years ago Brunner wanted to be one of those who would
build something new, something ignored and neglected
by the eighteenth and nineteenth centuries. Hence one
cannot but take it amiss that he has acted thus. He did
not hesitate to put forward a doctrine which he could
distinguish from that of St. Thomas only by setting it
over against a much distorted version of the latter. He
had no misgivings in proclaiming it as the very latest
thing and as the special task of our theological generation
that we should again walk in the way upon which
Protestant theology entered in the age of "rational
orthodoxy." He insisted on joining the most undesirable
figures of the Evangelical Germany of to-day (which are
not to be found among the "German Christians," but
half way between them and the confessional front). All
this is bad enough. But in comparing his own doctrine
with that of Calvin he should have received one last
shock, since he was faced with a conception which stands

in the strongest contrast to the ellipsis of his own thought.
For in Calvin's teaching God and his law, the mystery
of election, the incarnation and redemption, the Holy
Spirit as divine subject, Baptism and the Lord's Supper
as divine signs, justification and sanctification as divine
acts, are everything. Through the gift of revelation and
faith man as a rational creature is together with his
world miraculously *included* in these. But there is nothing
to justify his setting himself up over against them as the
propounder of a theme *of his own.* Hence also there is
nothing to justify an "other" task of theology. The substance of the Reformers' theology which is quite
unequivocal should have warned him, made him stop,
called him back. It should have reminded him of the
attitude of the biblical witnesses. It should have
reminded him that they uphold the idea that where God
speaks, man has to listen; where God gives, man has to
receive; where God acts, man has to be present *without*
considering his own importance (whether as natural or
as "pardoned" man)—*without* drawing arbitrary conclusions and thus translating the Word of God to man
into a word of man about himself and therefore *without*
proclaiming the *analogia entis* as a common "basis" of
Christian and pagan theology. It should have reminded
him that they uphold this idea to the exclusion of all
dialectic between nature and grace. Calvin's theology
should have challenged Brunner to use his great gifts
in the service of the task of working out and proclaiming
to-day the whole "one-sidedness" of the Reformers' conception over against a Roman Catholicism that has long
been renewed and refined and, above all, over against
the modernist Protestant flood which is to-day bursting
all dams. What Calvin wrote in those first chapters of
the *Institutes* has to be written again and this time in
such a way that no Przywara and no Althaus can find in
it material for their fatal ends. To do this would be to

"adhere to the teaching of the Reformation," and would at the same time be worthy of Brunner's own early intentions. But Brunner was not content merely to hunt with the hounds and to stab me in the back by telling *urbi et orbi* that the whole dispute was caused by *my* "one-sidedness." He has done more than that. Taking his position exactly where Calvin left the question open, he has gone and calmly claimed Calvin for his own; he has turned Calvin into a kind of Jean Alphonse Turrettini; he has confronted me together with his "Calvin" and has patted me on the shoulder and told me to be a good boy; he has seen to it that the "German Christians" can, if they wish—what will Mr. Stapel say to that?—quote now not only Luther but also Calvin in their support. It is the fact that he managed to do all these things which I am so far unable to forgive Brunner.

But Brunner's appeal to Calvin is in itself incapable of being upheld. Wherever I have followed up the references which he gives, I have found thoughts quite different from those of Brunner's text, which they are supposed to support. It will be the task of Peter Barth to elucidate this side of the matter, both as a whole and in detail. I shall here make but a few remarks, based on my limited knowledge of the subject:

(1) It is true that Calvin spoke of a *Duplex cognitio Domini*, from creation and in Christ (cf., *e.g.*, *Inst.*, I, ii, 1; Conf. Gall., 1559, Art. 2). But in contrast to Brunner he said about a natural knowledge of God through creation only what is said about it in Romans i, 19 f.; ii, 14 f.; Acts xiv, 15 f.; xvii, 24 f. He did not regard it as a capacity which man has retained and which has to be reconstituted by faith, as a point of contact for revelation and for the new life in Christ. Those passages, the Mosaic creation-narrative and Psalms 19 and 104 did not move him as a Christian to search in reason, history and nature for another source of revelation beside

Scripture, for one that would supplement Scripture.
Nor did he follow that up by allowing it to speak, at
least in a supplementary function, as an authority
"somehow" possessing an independent status. As with
all theologians both of old times and new, one has
constantly to ask how far he allowed his exegesis to be
positively influenced by considerations other than those
derived from the texts. But it is undeniable that he did
not try to justify such action systematically, that he
allowed neither to Christians nor to pagans any source
of revelations other than Holy Scripture, and that his
theology was as a matter of principle only interpretation
of Scripture and not also anthropology and philosophy
of history and nature.

(2) The possibility of a real knowledge by natural
man of the true God, derived from creation, is, according
to Calvin, a possibility in principle, but not in fact,
not a possibility to be realised by us. One might call
it an objective possibility, created by God, but not a
subjective possibility, open to man. Between what is
possible in principle and what is possible in fact there
inexorably lies the fall. Hence this possibility can only
be discussed hypothetically: *si integer stetisset* Adam
(*Inst.*, I, ii, 1). Man does not merely in part not have
this possibility; he does not have it at all. "We are
blind, not because revelation is obscure, but because
we are mad (*mente alienati*): we lack not only the will
but also the ability for this matter" (Comm. in 1 Cor.
i, 21; C.R. xlix, 326). That is true also of those "whose
eyes have been opened by Christ"! I cannot find any
passage which shows that Calvin followed up his discussion in the introduction to the *Institutes* of the
Platonic and Ciceronian philosophoumena concerning
God, the world and man, by maintaining a *natural*
knowledge, rectified by faith in Christ. Over against
the philosophers he sets the teaching of *Scripture* and

nothing else. Scripture tells him that man is created by God and for God, that the wisdom and paternal providence of God rules over his life and that of the whole world, that there are ordinances of God and what those ordinances are, in which he has to honour the will of God. Scripture moves and inspires him to praise through the creation the God who is so completely hidden from man. That is what man, who is reconciled in Christ, can and must do. He cannot and must not, however, embark upon independent speculations concerning these things, made apart from and without Holy Scripture or arbitrarily deduced from it.

(3) The possibility which, according to Calvin, man in fact has, is to know and worship the gods of his own heart: "The knowledge of God which now remains to man is nothing other than the terrible source of all idolatry and superstition" (Comm. in John iii, 6; C.R. xlvii, 57). It is quite impossible to see how this possibility could in Calvin's theology gain the status and significance of a "point of contact." Between it and the possibility of divine revelation there is no relation, nothing common, and hence no inner connection. "Guided by their reason they do not come to God, yea, they do not even approach him" (Comm. in John i, 5; C.R. xlvii, 5 f.). "If true religion is to beam upon us, our principle must be that it is necessary to begin with heavenly teaching (a coelesti doctrina) and that it is impossible for any man to obtain even the minutest portion of right and sound doctrine without being a disciple of Scripture. Hence the first step in true knowledge is taken when we reverently embrace the testimony, which God has been pleased therein to give of himself. For not only does faith, full and perfect faith, but all correct knowledge of God, originate in obedience" (Instit., I, vi, 2. Beveridge's transl.). In accordance with this the important transitional passage between

Instit., I, v and vi, says nothing about any manipulation that might in any way be regarded as a "point of contact." If one wanted a term to describe what is said at that point, it would rather have to be "repulsion." And it is a repulsion of a kind that cannot subsequently be re-interpreted as a contact!

(4) Calvin always used the idea of the possibility in principle of a "natural" knowledge of God (objectively based on the fact that God is revealed in all his works) in the sense of Romans i, 20, or rather in the sense of the whole passage, Romans i, 18-iii, 20. It serves to demonstrate the fact that man is without excuse. The fact that God is revealed in all his works is God's scriptural testimony to us against the ignorance of man. It justifies the wrath of God and his judgment upon man. It points out that man's inability to know him is his guilt. But it does not serve "to praise our perverted nature" (Comm. in John i, 5, *loc. cit.*). We cannot make anything of it. It is a fact that our ability to distinguish good and evil convicts us of our guilt. But Calvin did not, any more than St. Paul in his Epistle to the Romans, draw from this the systematic conclusion that a "natural" knowledge of the law of God is to be ascribed to us and that this knowledge has to be put to a positive use in theology *either* antecedently *or* subsequently ("in faith"). On the contrary, he plainly denied that knowledge of the ethical good is gained by means of an ability (*facultas*) of man. He described it as a daily renewed *beneficium*, even in the case of the regenerate (*Instit.*, II, ii, 25). There is really no need of any special exegetical virtuosity to see that in *Instit.*, II, xviii-xxv we are in quite a different world from that of Brunner's doctrine of the *imago*.

(5) It is true that, according to Calvin, the knowledge of God in Christ includes a real knowledge of the true God in creation. Includes! This means that it does not, as Brunner seems to think, bring forth a second, relatively

independent kind of knowledge, so that the circle would become an ellipsis after all—as if our reason, once it had been illumined, had of itself (*per se*) gained the power of sight (*Instit.*, II, ii, 25)! Calvin does not mean that room should be made after all for a Christian philosophy of nature and history, a Christian anthropology and psychology, a Christian—enthusiastic interpretation of our times! Calvin says: "*Christ* is the *imago* in which God makes manifest to us not only his heart but also his hands and his feet." But Calvin knows no abstraction from this subject: "As soon as we depart from Christ there is no matter great or small in which we would not give way to our own imaginations." Knowledge of God from creation comes to Moses, not by free speculation but strictly in view of the history of salvation (*historia instaurationis*), *i.e.* of the foundation, preservation and government of the Church (Preface to the Comm. in Gen. C.R. xxiii, 10 f.). Those passages of Calvin (like those passages of Scripture!), where the Reformer consciously and as a matter of principle wanted something different, where what he says about God in nature and history is meant to be anything but (materially) the proclamation of Christ and (formally) exegesis of Scripture—those passages have yet to be found.

Brunner's interpretation of Calvin has one fault which vitiates everything. He has, with amazing cold blood and consistency, left out the very important brackets within which Calvin always speaks of the natural knowledge of God. They are the expression *si integer stetisset* Adam, which makes it a hypothetical possibility, the reference to Romans i, 20, which makes it a sign of the judgment, Christ and the Church as the place which must not be abandoned if it wants to be understood also as a sign of grace. By means of leaving all this out, Brunner has brought Calvin over to his side. Also, in detail, the whole process is enough to make one weep.

V

BRUNNER THEN AND NOW

BRUNNER is of the opinion that "it can easily be seen from what Calvin says concerning this subject (eristics) how far this is possible by way of *theologia naturalis.*" Indeed it is generally not difficult to see what he is up to. But there is one special question to be asked and in any case a caution to be issued.

If *Nature and Grace* were the only pronouncement we had from Brunner on the subject of *theologia naturalis*, we should think that we were dealing with a representative of the *"rational orthodoxy"* of the late seventeenth or early eighteenth century who had risen again and was speaking to us in modern terms. I am thinking of that very influential school of thought whose leaders were mostly very serious people and which was then felt by a wide public to be taking a great step towards freedom. Its representatives in Germany were Buddeus and Pfaff, in Switzerland J. A. Turrettini, Osterwald and Werenfels. The growth of the pietistic movement and the general advance in education had woken them from the slumber of mere theological intellectualism and with an aim *ad praxin pietatis* in doctrine as well, they tried to achieve a pious and sensible alliance between revelation and reason. In discussing the history of dogma Brunner mentions the Enlightenment and Rationalism—but why not this interesting intermediary period in which took place the essential or at least the open transition from the old Protestantism to Neo-Protestantism, with regard to the problem of nature and grace? Does he not know it? Or if he does know it, where does he propose to draw the dividing line between himself and these "spirits of moderation"? What is it that Brunner's *Nature and Grace* does? The genius of one-sidedness is called to account by means of that very useful distinction between the material *imago Dei* in man, which has been lost, and the formal *imago Dei* which has not. Brunner states that man recognises an independent revelation of God in creation. Of course it is recognised "in all its magnitude" only by those "whose eyes have been opened by Christ," but the others know it too, though only "to some extent." Nothing now seems to prevent us; rather are we invited, by what has been said "from Calvin's point of view," to look quite simply and directly for "the original creation, in so far as it is still recognisable as such"; for "the God-given form of all created being"; for "the will of God imprinted upon all existence from creation"; for man's "experience of his preserving and providential grace" as "an important complement of the knowledge of God derived from Scripture"; for the *lex naturae* which merely needs to be brought out again through Scripture, *i.e.* for the "ordinances of creation and nature" that have been only somewhat obscured by sin; for the *humanum*, and finally for the rational nature of man as the *imago Dei*. According to *Nature and Grace* we should have to assume that these are all discoverable and demonstrable data— "only up to a certain degree never capable of being accurately fixed." Nevertheless it can be fixed! According to Brunner the task of our theological generation is to find the way back to a "true *theologia naturalis.*" And after what has been said "from Calvin's point of view," the programme of this theology seems to be given by a catalogue of all that is capable of being determined within the suggested limits. The theologians of two hundred years ago were equally far removed from the extremes of Rationalism and the Enlightenment. They were even further removed, fundamentally removed, from the "one-sidedness" with which the orthodoxy of the seventeenth century had tried to derive theological truths only from the Holy Scriptures, given and interpreted by the Holy Spirit. They had the same boldness, tempered by prudence, the same piety tempered by morality, and with these they tried in that period of transition to build a new bridge between revelation and reason, faith and life, Church and culture. If that is Brunner's programme, and if he succeeds in carrying it out, then we are without doubt in a strange time, when the history of modern theology shows itself to be a complete circle. We have, then, to expect a new Christian Wolff, a new Semler, a new Lessing, and at last a new Schleiermacher, each in his own time, before the end of the twentieth century. Then we would have a repetition of all the mishaps of the nineteenth century until, at the beginning of the twenty-second, we should again be more or less where we are now! Joking apart, was there no good spirit to warn Brunner, when he had that idea about the distinction between the material and the formal *imago*, that he was thereby adopting the classical scheme of thought of the eighteenth century? And will our poor Protestantism come safely through a second revolution through 360 degrees, which Brunner's programme, based on this distinction, seems inevitably to announce?

But the question concerning Brunner's "true" *theologia naturalis*, of which we have already spoken, is the following: Does he really mean a *theologia naturalis* consisting of propositions and instruction directly obtained from natural evidence, of the kind that was introduced into Protestant theology two hundred years ago? *Nature and Grace* would lead one to suppose so. But against this there is Brunner's *last* authoritative pronouncement *but one* on the subject, which seems (at least at the first glance) to point in a somewhat different direction. In the article, "Die Frage nach dem 'Anknüpfungspunk' als Problem der Theologie" ("The question of the 'point of contact' as a theological problem," *Zwischen den Zeiten*, 1932, pp. 505 ff.), he gave his doctrine a turn which is now conspicuously absent. But there has been no explicit retractation, so that we have to reckon with the possibility of its reappearing again one day. It seemed, then, that Brunner was not speaking, as he is now, of a directly observable continuity between nature and grace, reason and revelation, but of a continuity which at the same time was discontinuity, which provided both a contact and a contrast. The latter was said to be so great that the continuity was subordinate to the discontinuity, the contact to the contrast. "The Gospel cannot be preached unless this continuity is completely disrupted. The content of the Gospel is of such a kind that by it this previous understanding (*i.e.* of God through reason) is not merely corrected but decidedly negatived. The natural knowledge of God is neither a true knowledge of *God* nor a true *knowledge* of God" (p. 510 f.). All natural knowledge of God is—so Brunner then said—essentially a knowledge of the wrath of God. And being subject to the wrath of God meant the same thing objectively as a bad conscience or despair subjectively. The different degrees of the subjective consciousness point to the objective side. The "contact" made in the natural knowledge of God consists in the fact that it involves a "loss of certainty." The contact is made, not with something positive or neutral but with something negative. As regards the contents of the relations of God and man there is a discontinuity. Only as regards the formal fact of the relation is there continuity (p. 523 f.). Hence the proclamation of the God revealed in Christ must always be at the same time an attempt "to show to the unbeliever the true character of his existence without faith, to show that despair is the 'fundamental condition' of existence." "Humanly

H

speaking, the success of the preaching of the Gospel is
as dependent upon the contact that is made as upon true
doctrine. And this contact consists of leading man to
the place where he will know the desperate character of
his existence, not merely theoretically but in his conscience." For "bringing into captivity every thought to
the obedience of Christ" (2 Cor. x, 5) means "that man
recognises himself in what is said to him by Christ
concerning his natural existence, so that he can identify
himself with it." Similarly, theology has to make
contact with the natural self-knowledge of man by
elucidating and underlining its negative result from the
point of view of faith. "Eristic theology means 'laying
bare' the true character of existence by destroying the
fictions of every *Weltanschauung*. But this 'laying bare'
cannot be performed except by using what man can of
himself know about himself" (p. 529 f.).

That *used to be* Brunner's opinion. Evidently he was
going to model his natural theology on the famous
examples of Kierkegaard and Heidegger. But in *Nature
and Grace* there is a remarkable silence in that quarter,
although faint echoes of the idea may be discernible in
the doctrine of the formal and material *imago*. The word
"capacity for revelation," which has now become so
significant, was absent then. Perhaps that has something
to do with it. The question is this: has Brunner abandoned that merely indirect or negative significance of
the natural knowledge of God? The disappearance of
this matter is to be regretted, at least in the interest of
the information of the public. Brunner's theory was very
much more interesting in its earlier form, in accordance
with Kierkegaard and Heidegger. For, in spite of its
restrained formulation, it raised the problem of a peculiar
aptitude of man for divine revelation in a much more
acute, tempting and dangerous form. I confess that
around 1920, and perhaps even later, I might still have

succumbed to it. And who knows whether one could not find passages in the *Epistle to the Romans* in which I have said something of the sort myself. According to Brunner's former explanation, man's aptitude for the revelation of God consists only in the fact that in the rational existence of man there is a diacritical point where this existence can become discontinuous, where it can issue in a "negative point," where its most essential truth, its "fundamental condition," *i.e.* despair, can come to light, where this despair can be theoretically described as true and felt to be so by the conscience, and where the knowledge of God, which is bound up with it from the start, can "become uncertain." Formal and material humanity are apparently still contrasted quite sharply and incompatibly, like continuity and discontinuity or the conditioned and unconditioned (p. 525). The ability of reason is only its ability to be negated. All that man "can do" with reference to revelation is to despair. Nor did Brunner fail to add that the transition from the *ability* to despair to *real* despair is dependent on grace. Accordingly the independent functions of natural theology would be the following: theology and proclamation of the Gospel must not confine themselves to putting forward "true doctrine." In, with and under the preaching of revelation, natural theology would have to use what man can of himself know concerning himself. It would have to tell him about himself, *i.e.* about his deepest despair of himself. Lastly, it would have to use the demonstration of this negative point to destroy all the fictions of *Weltanschauungen*. Again we may ask: why was Brunner silent about *these* things in 1934? Why did he not leave it at *that*? Why has the car got out of hand and run down to the plain where it is now much easier to make it stop? What is the slope that seems to have made it run irresistibly from one place to the other?

However that may be, it is our duty to apply the brakes

to the car before it runs down the slope, although that may be more difficult. We have to *prevent* it from running down, right into the *theologia naturalis vulgaris*, where we find it to-day in Brunner's case. The "No!" with which we have to oppose Brunner applies even if he should one day return to the form of his doctrine which follows Kierkegaard and Heidegger. There is no fundamental difference between that form and the one which he seems to wish to adopt now. They both maintain that man has a "capacity for revelation"—there is no reason why Brunner should not have used that term even then. It has to be opposed even in that more refined form, which seems to touch Evangelical truth with great precision and which, therefore, is all the more dangerous. Brunner's conception of the Roman Catholic doctrine is insufficient and not authoritative. If he had derived his information from the works of E. Przywara he would have found that this great exponent of the doctrine of analogy long ago used a phrase of the fourth Lateran Council and also the whole Kierkegaardian dialectic to interpret the ability to despair and real despair in a Roman Catholic sense. For Przywara maintains that this correlation is included and preserved in the Augustinian-Thomist scheme of *natura, gratia praeveniens* and *gratia gratum faciens*. He not only did but he *could* justifiably interpret it in a Roman Catholic sense.

In speaking of a "destruction of all the fictions of *Weltanschauungen*," of making the knowledge of God "uncertain" and turning it into a knowledge of the wrath of God, of the demonstration of the desperate character of our existence, etc., Brunner was stating a real theological problem. But this theological problem is put to us by the truth, presented in the Scriptures, Creeds and Confessions, that man is of himself unable to find access to the revelation of God. Just because Christ is born, we have to regard the world as lost in the

sight of God. The Word of God declares man to be
unfree in his relations with God. The fact that we become
hearers and doers of the Word of God signifies the
realisation of a divine possibility, not of one that is
inherent in our human nature. Freedom to know the
true God is a miracle, a freedom of God, not one of our
freedoms. Faith in the revelation of God makes this
negation inevitable. To contradict it would amount to
unbelief. But as early as 1932 Brunner showed that he
had not absorbed this piece of insight in the way in
which it is presented to us. Otherwise he could not
possibly have again at this point spoken of a "natural"
knowledge of God. Nor could he possibly have said that
the state of affairs to which this knowledge relates could
be seen only by "utilising that which man can of himself
know about himself." How can man ever in any sense
know "of himself" what has to be known here? He may
know it *himself, yes*! But "of himself," never! How could
he possibly convince himself of this negation of his
freedom? He could only do it if he thought that he could,
in advance, overlook and grasp both the Word of God
and himself, if he thought not only that he knew the
condition of his hearing of the Word—*i.e.* the negation of
his freedom to do so—but also that he could create it
himself. If we base ourselves upon what is possible to
us, we shall always *believe* in these our possibilities and
always *have* to believe in them. Hence we shall not *be
able* to destroy "the fictions of *Weltanschauungen.*" The
power to rid ourselves of these fictions and of the illusion
of our freedom which underlies them, is in no sense our
power, but solely the power of the Word itself. And in
so far as this happens to ourselves it is the power of the
Holy Spirit. All the comfort, all the power, all the
truth of the revelation of God depends on the fact that
it is God who is thus revealed to us. And all understanding of this fact of revelation depends on its identity

with God being understood, on all possibilities except
that of God being excluded. This applies also, or even
specially, to the "loss of certainty"! Also the *wrath* of
God is the wrath of *God*. Hence it is by no means
identical with any fundamental condition or "negative
point" of our existence. The presence of *Yahweh* is
necessary to make man say, "Woe is me! for I am
undone" (Is. vi, 5). "The Spirit of the Lord bloweth
upon it," *therefore* the grass withers and the flower fades
(Is. xl, 7). The world cannot reprove itself, but according
to John xvi, 8 f., it is the *Holy Spirit*, the Comforter, that
will reprove it. Similarly we "can" not of ourselves pass
through the strait gate or enter upon the narrow way
(Matt. vii, 14). We do not of ourselves "become as little
children" (Matt. xviii, 3), nor are we of ourselves "born
again" (John iii, 3). In the same way not even the
starting-point of the way "from death to life" (John v, 24;
1 John iii, 14) lies within the sphere of what is possible
to us. For not only the resurrection and the life, but
also the death, perishing and putting off of the old man
(Luke xv, 32; Romans viii, 10; 2 Cor. iv, 16; Col. iii, 9 f.;
Eph. ii, 5; 2 Tim. ii, 11) which precede and underlie
them, take place once and for all *in Christ* (Romans
vi, 3 f.; 2 Cor. v, 14; Phil. iii, 10 f.) and are made fruitful
for us in the *Holy Spirit* (Gal. v, 16; Romans viii, 13).
According to Luther, man is not a "sinner" by nature.
He has to *become* one, and it is "a rare thing and a
hard one" to become a sinner (Comm. on Romans
1515/16, Ficker II, lxxi, 1 f.). "As the righteousness of
God lives in us through *faith*, so it is also with sin; that
is, we must *believe* that we are sinners" (lxix, 10). "We
have to give way to his *revelation*, that is to his *Words*, to
justify and confirm them, and thus on the basis of what
they say to us to confess to ourselves what we did not
know before, namely that we are sinners" (lxvii, 31).
Humilitas can exist only as *spiritualitas* (cxlv, 23). Hence

only the *spiritual* man can speak of himself as St. Paul does in Romans vii (cxlvii, 32). If anyone is incapable of glorying in his own power, this is a sign of *election* (ccxxix, 21; ccxlix, 12). According to Calvin, true knowledge of self in real humility cannot precede the knowledge of God, it must follow the latter. We perceive how little our eyes are able to bear the light, not when we direct them on to the ground, but when we try to look at the sun (*Instit.*, I, 1). Therefore it is not the case that the continuity of our human understanding could by some inherent necessity turn into discontinuity and that therefore our understanding could, thanks to the possibility of its negation, somehow turn "of itself" into an understanding of divine revelation. Nor are we dealing with an order which, on the basis of some synthetic piece of insight, might just as well be reversed. It does not matter whether the despair which we experience and know as our own is, according to one philosophy, the "fundamental condition" of our existence or, according to another, something else. At any rate *that* despair is not a factor which co-operates with the judgment of God and which, therefore, is indispensable for its execution. Nor is it, as Brunner evidently thought and still thinks, indirectly identical with the judgment of God, as being its subjective manifestation. *That* sorrow which really is possible to us is always that sorrow of which it is said in 2 Cor. vii, 10, that it "worketh death." It may be "shown up." But what can here be shown up and appear can never be the sorrow "after a godly manner" which works "repentance not to be repented of," which leads to salvation. Not even when it is in the sphere of grace! On the contrary, even when it enters into the sphere of grace I have to realise that in *that* sorrow which *I* experience, undergo and know as *my own*, I am still, and even all the more, my own lord and master. *That* "loss of certainty" of the natural knowledge of God, *that* destruction of the "fictions of *Weltanschauungen*" which I can with my little piece of despair undertake and carry out, is bound to issue in the erection of the worst of all idols, namely a so-called "truth," from the throne of which *I* consider myself able to see through all gods and to unmask them as idols. The better I succeed in despairing, the more certainly this must be the end. The world which *I* have cleared of gods is truly neither the kingdom of the living God nor even a preparation for it, but probably the worst of all forms of diabolism, by which I can oppose that kingdom. What has this grasping after the judgeship of the world in common with the obedience of Christ of 2 Corinthians x, 5? Where is every thought brought into captivity? Does it not triumph all the more in unmitigated hybris? Is there any form of pride worse than that of a certain type of Kierkegaardianism? Has there ever been a more explicit Prometheanism than that of the philosophy of an existence despairing of itself? How can that "negative point" be the "point of contact" for divine revelation, since its demonstration leads necessarily to a triumph of reason at its most natural and unregenerate? If our preaching is going to be dependent upon the success of that kind of "contact" it is hardly going to be "true doctrine." Even at this stage it becomes evident that the distinction between the formal and the material personality of man and therefore also that between the continuity and the discontinuity of our existence is impracticable. If anyone knows of a diacritical point, where *gratia praeveniente* continuity and discontinuity can be one, he is evidently thinking of discontinuity from the point of view of an unreal continuity or of continuity from the point of view of an unreal discontinuity. He knows *continuity* only as conditioned by discontinuity and *discontinuity* as a solution of the problem of continuity. Also the equation of this contrast with that between the

conditioned and the unconditioned only goes to show
that he is thinking of a reversible and therefore im-
manent, theologically irrelevant contrast. What he calls
the purely formal side of humanity is evidently full of
material. And the material is the capacity for a sinless
knowledge of sin, the capacity to do on earth subjectively,
per analogiam, what God does in heaven *per essentiam,*
i.e. to sit in judgment on human existence, to inform
oneself concerning oneself, to know oneself to be punished
with despair, to destroy the fictions of *Weltanschauungen,*
to unmask idols, etc. If that isn't capacity for revelation . . .! Again we may say: Brunner might just as
well have used that word in 1932! One may guess the
scruples he then had against doing so. But one can also
understand that these scruples could and finally must
disappear as being unnecessary. One can understand
that he could not stop at a merely negative definition
of the "point of contact." "If the cloak falls, the duke
must needs follow." The "point of contact" had now
to be defined positively in the same way in which it was
then defined negatively. Hence full scope is given to the
theologia naturalis vulgaris and we begin to move again
round the circle in which theology evidently has moved
for two hundred years. This depressing result could be
achieved even via Kierkegaard. The doctrine of the
point of contact and the whole of Brunner's teaching on
nature and grace, even in its earlier forms and irrespective
of its later developments, has to be most categorically
opposed on the score that it is incompatible with the third
article of the creed. The Holy Ghost, who proceeds
from the Father and the Son and is therefore revealed
and believed to be God, does not stand in need of any
point of contact but that which he himself creates. Only
retrospectively is it possible to reflect on the way in which
he "makes contact" with man, and this retrospect will
ever be a retrospect upon a *miracle.*

VI

BRUNNER'S AIM

I THINK that I do not misunderstand Brunner if I regard what he says under the heading, "The significance of *theologia naturalis* for theology and the Church," as the core of his essay and of his whole undertaking. And again I do not think that I misunderstand him in putting in the following order of interest and urgency the things he means when he says "theology and the Church": he wishes to carry on pastoral work among intellectuals, to instruct modern youth, to carry on the discussion with the unbelievers. He wishes to be a Christian pedagogue in the widest sense of the word, a preacher, a moralist, and lastly also a dogmatic theologian. No doubt this describes my sphere of duty as well, and "somehow" also that of every theologian active in the Church and in the academic pursuits which she requires—though I am of the opinion that the order ought to be somewhat different.

Again there exists no difference between Brunner and myself in that in our activity, both as a whole and in detail, we are constantly faced with the double question: *what* has to be done? and: *how* is it to be done? It is the question concerning content and that concerning language, the question concerning revelation and the question what I and my audience and readers ought to "make of it." But we are not at one as soon as Brunner maintains that the two questions are on one level; that they are therefore comparable; that they can therefore be raised and answered while comfortably separated; and when he wishes to treat the question of method, of language, of form, separately. (He distinguishes the latter as the question of love from the question of faith!)

When Brunner thought it necessary (*Zwischen den Zeiten,* 1929, p. 255 f.) to proclaim "the *other* task of theology," I knew that we were not at one. For I fail to see how the abstraction which this title expresses is possible in theology. Consequently I also fail to see it in other contexts. If theology and human life in general is concerned with God, his Word, his acts and his rule, then the question of language and form is certainly as important as the unquestionable fact that it is we ourselves who are occupied by this matter in one way or another. But this means that it cannot be raised and answered except as a peripheral question, invalid and ever to be invalidated again. Nor can it be any care but a care cast upon God. How could it fail to be included in the one theme of theology? Why should it become a separate theme beside that one? How could it become a "decisive" matter? If Brunner and I did not, unfortunately, also differ concerning the dogma of the virgin birth, I should now ask him whether the question of Mary (Luke i, 34): "How shall this be, seeing I know not a man?" is a "decisive" question. Can this question have any weight *of its own*, any importance of its *own*, beside *the* question, to which the angel does actually give an answer in verse 35? Is it not included and preserved in the latter in the best manner possible?

The natural consequences of this first fundamental abstraction is that Brunner cannot dispense with natural theology. Whoever makes such an abstraction will inevitably get into some kind of natural theology. Brunner looks around in the sphere of theological and ecclesiastical activity and sees himself faced with the unquestionable fact that it is everywhere concerned with God. But it is concerned with God in the human sphere and therefore within the sphere of reference of the problems of human form and language. Probably one should not blame him for raising the question "How?"

when faced with this spectacle. For it corresponds to the question of Mary: "How shall these things be?" and also to the cry of the disciples: "Master, carest thou not that we perish?" (Mark iv, 38). But his answer to this question is not modelled on the *miraculous* continuation of these and many similar biblical stories. Why not? Why is the simple adherence to the *one* task of theology suddenly "individualism," "nominalism," "intellectualism," "one-sidedness"? Why does Brunner suddenly fear that it will be impossible to put forward "biblical or reformed ethics"? Why does he fear a "complete isolation of the Church" and evidently much else besides, such as, *e.g.*, to go to hell for "despising the question of the How"? What cares are these! And why on earth does he not offer to us, at all those points of the activity of the Church and her theology, a reminder of Mark ii, 9, "Arise, take up thy bed and walk!"? Instead he offers us his—oh, so feeble—"doctrine of the *imago Dei* and especially of responsibility" as our mainstay and bridge and comfort. " *The Church also is dependent upon the possibility of speaking to man of God at all.*" (Italics mine.) Is this what is meant by speaking out of faith, out of love, out of concentration upon one's objective, out of knowledge of the mystery of Christ? Where in the history or teaching of the Bible has Brunner found the slightest support for this sentence with the fatal word "also"? What Prophet, what apostle could—as far as he was true to his mission—hit upon the idea that he was dependent upon this "at all"? Does not this sentence betray a theory which thinks that as regards theological and ecclesiastical practice it must find help elsewhere than in the revelation of God—and thinks that it has already found it? If we base theological and ecclesiastical practice upon this sentence, do we not forget entirely that only God can be called to witness for God, that therefore the word of man cannot witness to the Word of

God? Is that sentence to be understood otherwise than
as a statement of human fear, wit and agility, which
thinks that it has to improve upon what God has done
well and will do well, which is chiefly concerned with
success and not the command, the promises, and the end?
Alas for the Church, of which what that sentence says
is true! Alas for the theologians, who in order to speak
of God truly and as Christians must first strive "to
speak of God at all"! Alas for the congregations, the
"intellectuals," the youth who sooner or later will only
hear "of God at all"! For when have things taken a
different course? Alas for the world, if in spite of the
birth, death and resurrection of Christ, "the Church
also" is "dependent" upon that!

In view of the fact that theological and ecclesiastical
practice is a human practice in the human sphere,
something quite, quite different would have to be said!
We should have to speak of the unconditional command
that has been issued in this sphere and is valid in it; of
the day of Jesus Christ, which makes this sphere a limited
sphere and at the same time a sphere of hope; of the
power unto victory inherent in the matter itself, for
which the Church is allowed to contend, succumbing
but never yielding an inch; of the confidence, of which
the Word and the Spirit of God and therefore also th :
Holy Scriptures and therefore the Sacraments, and
therefore also our weak and miserable preaching are
worthy, and which we owe to them, because they are
God or institutions of God; of the love which we show
to men, not by proffering them useless bridges and
crutches but by helping them to guard the sanctuary
of God upon earth, so that it shall remain a sanctuary
and as such a place of salvation; of the perseverance
with which this task has to be undertaken, ever anew and
ever more loyally, ever better known in its peculiarity.
Have we ever said enough of this? Has it ever been said

and heard to such an extent that we might at least have
sufficient time and energy left to turn to an "other" task of
theology? Do we ever leave the first task behind us, so that
from it we *could* move to some next item on the agenda?

But what of the How? I reply: assuming that we had
put our hands to the plough, could we look back?
Assuming we were really caught by the What, *i.e.*
arrested by that command, by the knowledge of that
limit and that hope, by the knowledge of that victorious
power, by the necessity of that confidence, conditioned
by the activity of that love and perseverance—could we
even for a moment seek the How outside the What?
Could it, even for a moment, become a "decisive"
question for us? The How am I myself, my audience
and readers, our time, with its convictions and illusions,
the cosmos of nature and history. In short, it is man,
in whose sphere there exist, among other things, theology
and the Church. But man is a being that has to be
overcome by the Word and the Spirit of God, that
has to be reconciled to God, justified and sanctified,
comforted and ruled and finally saved by God. Is that
not enough? Is not every addition to that really a
subtraction from it? Would theology and the Church
honour man if they demanded something "decisive"
from him *as well*—a second decisive factor, a second or
first revelation? No doubt the question "How?" will
always be constituted by man, by human nature, language
and form. It will certainly be preserved. The creation
and preserving patience of God will see to it that this
little monster in me and in others and in our whole
common sphere is not deprived of its rights. Does this
mean that the question "How?" can and may be heard
independently, as conveying a "natural knowledge of
God"? What has man, that he has not received? Are
not both he and the question "How?" included and
preserved in the "What?", which alone is decisive: in

the fact that Christ has died and risen for man? We
not theology and the Church dishonour man if they
addressed him, not because he *has been addressed* but
because he *can be addressed*? By so doing they would
question or even deny the one all-important positive
good thing that can be said about him. And that they
ought not to do. It is not a practical thing to be so
unpractical for the sake of a practice.

And what of pastoral work and teaching and preaching, of pedagogy, ethics and dogmatics? And the *success*
which Brunner evidently has in view in the argument of
the last part of his essay? We all work for success and
not for failure, and if the question is put in its right place
and duly bracketed, we may say something about it:

In my experience the best way of dealing with "unbelievers" and modern youth is not to try to bring out
their "capacity for revelation," but to treat them
quietly, simply (remembering that Christ has died and
risen also for them), as if their rejection of "Christianity"
was not to be taken seriously. It is only then that they
can understand you, since they really see you where you
maintain that you are standing as an evangelical
theologian: on the ground of justification by faith alone.

I have the impression that my sermons reach and
"interest" my audience most when I least rely on
anything to "correspond" to the Word of God already
"being there," when I least rely on the "possibility" of
proclaiming this Word, when I least rely on my ability to
"reach" people by my rhetoric, when on the contrary I
allow my language to be formed and shaped and adapted
as much as possible by what the text seems to be saying.

I should consider Christian education, in the wide
sense of the word in which Brunner is thinking of it, a
hopeful undertaking if it did not base itself upon any
"pedagogic factor," but began at the beginning and
considered the "education" of man by the Word of God.

Ethics will be quite a good and useful thing if it always remembers the commandments of God. In contrast to Brunner's ethics it should not be based on a dogmatic presupposition of those mythical "ordinances." Therefore it should refrain from trying to turn the commandments of God into the commandments of men.

Finally, dogmatics will be the better and the more instructive, the more it keeps to the rule of Hilary: *Non sermoni res, sed rei sermo subjectus est*—the less it looks for an already existing "aptitude" of certain analogies. Brunner has tried to prove that in my own dogmatics I practise the opposite. Let the reader decide whether he is right. It was certainly not done purposely or consciously. Moreover, the "important passage" which Brunner quotes to support this contention does not bear that meaning in its context. Brunner has misquoted it, evidently having misread it and left out a clause.

I should like to call the theological and ecclesiastical "successes" which might be attained in this direction "*spiritual*" and "*interesting*." Those that may no doubt be attained in the opposite direction I should call "*unspiritual*" and "*uninteresting*."

It will be best to conclude by explicitly moving away once more from this quite secondary and *un*important question. We are not here at all in order to gather successes. We are commanded to do work that has a reason and foundation. *That* is why there is hope in that work. Natural theology is always the answer to a question which is false if it wishes to be "decisive." That is the question concerning the "How?" of theological and ecclesiastical activity. Hence it has to be rejected *a limine*—right at the outset. Only the theology and the church of the antichrist can profit from it. The Evangelical Church and Evangelical theology would only sicken and die of it.

Made in the USA
Middletown, DE
19 September 2018